SOAKED IN JOY

BOOK8 REFLECTIONS OF GOD MOMENTS

Dedication

To all who have soaked my life in richness with your touch, your wisdom and your experiences. To Kelley Inderman for being a true blessing in editing and partnership to make this process so much easier, thank you is not enough! To Will Baten who has continued to strive to capture the essence of my thoughts and translate into beautiful artwork, God bless you greatly! To my friends, family, colleagues and employees who have contributed so richly to my life, I am completely washed in your love and gratitude no words are good enough to express my appreciation.

Soaked in Joy
Book 8 Reflections of God Moments
copyright © 2024

Written by: Donesa Walker
Design by: Will Baten
Edited by: Kelley Inderman

"Who do you think will feel sorry for you, Jerusalem?
Who do you think will waste tears on you?
Who will bother to take the time to ask,
'So, how are things going?'
"You left me, remember?" God's Decree.
"You turned your back and walked out.
So I will grab you and hit you hard.
I'm tired of letting you off the hook.
I threw you to the four winds
and let the winds scatter you like leaves.
I made sure you'll lose everything,
since nothing makes you change.
I created more widows among you
than grains of sand on the ocean beaches.
At noon mothers will get the news
of their sons killed in action.
Sudden anguish for the mothers—
all those terrible deaths.
A mother of seven falls to the ground,
gasping for breath,
Robbed of her children in their prime.
Her sun sets at high noon!
Then I'll round up any of you that are left alive
and see that you're killed by your enemies."
God's Decree.

Jeremiah 15: 5-9

God's Decree!

I have wrestled with this all night and all morning because my heart is so heavy. I attended a local event last night, which is a huge event in our area, and it was beautiful, but oh, my heart broke as I looked around and saw so many completely lost people. I felt a little like Jesus did on that mountain as He saw the hurting and broken. Here were hundreds of people who had spent lots of money on outfits, hairdos and jewelry to attend a gala event that people had spent thousands of hours putting together and yet the rampant sin was evident everywhere. Inebriated people socialized while bidding on pieces of art and jewelry as well as other items like trips and such. Scantily clad women and men dressed as women gyrated on stages to pounding music while oglers looked on. I left. I could not stay and see this show at the expense of so many as I know the intent was for a good cause but the shame of it overwhelmed me. The beautiful decor and incredible arrangement of items for bid was overshadowed by the bars flowing with liquor and men tucking money into places lacking clothing. I'm sure the majority of those who attended would say it was a resounding success and that it raised money for a good cause, but I felt oily and heavy with grief for the incredible lack of shame. On the flip side, I had experienced an incredible experience of relaxation and love at my staff party earlier that day. We sat in a quiet, secluded restaurant on their last day of business celebrating the love of each other and the clients we get the opportunity to pour into daily. We prayed together and blessed each other. The extreme of the one to the other was like cold water. One event of sweet anointing had cost less for all of us than the attendance of one person to the other event of embarrassing shame. None of this is to put anyone down or criticize but rather exacted the same feeling Jeremiah had in the prophecy in chapter 15. Who do you think will waste tears or feel sorry for us or even take the time to ask how things are going when we so openly have deserted God? God's decree says He is tired of this blatant refusal to acknowledge Him and the way we continue to turn towards sin. He says He will grab us hard and shake us as He is tired of us turning our backs and walking off without a care in the world until we need Him. He says He has given us more windows or chances than the grains of sand on the ocean beaches but nothing makes us change. Oh how heavy my heart is that I mourn America in her heartland openly defying the Creator of all mankind. The glitz and glamor will turn to mourning. In Jeremiah, he says mothers will have sudden anguish as their sons are killed in action; robbed of their children, gasping for breath as all of their loved ones are ripped from their arms. Oh America....can you not see? Judgment is coming...oh that we would repent and turn.

"I don't think the way you think. The way you work isn't the way I work." God's Decree. "For as the sky soars high above earth, so the way I work surpasses the way you work, and the way I think is beyond the way you think.

Just as rain and snow descend from the skies and don't go back until they've watered the earth, Doing their work of making things grow and blossom, producing seed for farmers and food for the hungry, So will the words that come out of my mouth not come back empty-handed. They'll do the work I sent them to do, they'll complete the assignment I gave them.
Isaiah 55:8-11

Empty Handed!

Sometimes I just don't understand the thinking of my husband. He finds sitting and watching a fire burn on TV relaxing while it frustrates me because nothing is happening. Men and women don't think alike and neither does God think like us. We are finite, limited and bound by Earth's constraints except in extreme situations like taking a rocket to the moon but God is infinite, unlimited and not bound by any force as He is God. In Isaiah, God says that He doesn't think or work the way that we do because what He sees, does, thinks is way beyond our imaginings. His words have power to enact change and will not return to Him until they have done as He commanded. Light meant that light would be born and continue to be born until He declares it over. Stars are born every day because His word Light is still working. You may not see His word evident in you but I promise it is. His promises are secure and backed by Him which is much more secure than the paper dollar backed by a little gold which He created. The dollar may fall, the world may fail us, people may disappoint us and life may feel frustrating but God's word is still alive and working. Joseph had a dream as a child which led to a lot of unhappy circumstances in his life but ultimately the dream he had came about because God had promised him in a dream. He had to wait years and I am sure that he felt lost and wondering a lot during that time in prison and in other situations but God's word was still working behind the scenes. His ways are not ours and we must have peace in that. He says that in this world we have troubles but to be of good cheer because He has overcome this world. The picture behind this scripture is one that means a lot to me as it is from a sweet young lady who is a talented artist that I have invested into for now. She has so much potential that I see but she rarely sees that for herself because when you are in the mixing, it's hard to see the beauty of the result. I especially love the clouds in this portrait because they depict the serenity of God as He looks down upon us as little flowers being tossed to and fro. We may sometimes be a taller flower among the others leading the way but easily a storm in life can knock us down making us less than we once were. We can see that as a loss or as a chance to go to seed and spread ourselves into others so that they can blossom and grow replicating the process of who God intends us to be. The truth is we are born naked and empty handed and we will leave here naked and empty handed. In the interim, our job is to be what He wants us to be using our empty hands to pick up the broken and down trodden to bring them to the Master. There He will take what we bring and make something priceless. I could buy the same tools and paints and canvases as this young lady did and I could attempt to paint this photo but I cannot for that is not the talent that God gave me. He gave me something different and I will use it for His glory because what He sends out does not come back empty handed. Take your empty hand and put it into His nail scarred one. Then you will be filled with abundant life and suddenly your empty hands become hands of power and might through His words.

And now, God, do it again—
bring rains to our
drought-stricken lives
So those who planted their
crops in despair
will shout "Yes!" at the harvest,
So those who went off with
heavy hearts
will come home laughing, with
armloads of blessing.

Psalms 126: 4-6

Armloads of Blessings!

Drought-anguish-grief all have something in common called despair. Despair is the loss of hope. Jesus said He came that we might have Life and Hope abundantly. Titus 2:13 and 1 Timothy 1:1 both tell us that Jesus is our Blessed Hope! When drought comes, the trees drop leaves and scale back preparing to weather the lack of water. The roots begin to go down seeking groundwater and gaining deeper access to underground sources. They understand that their source of water isn't coming from the surroundings and they must dig a little deeper. Planting crops in drought is seen as foolish as it appears that there is no purpose-no growth to happen but God is that hope and source. Right now, with a pall of despair over the country from economic woes and political wars as well as extreme uncertainty and frustration, it is hard to have hope. Many are walking about depressed and in complete despair. Mental health workers are overwhelmed with the extreme needs from young children to adults. David is calling upon God in this passage to Do It Again! It is what God does to bring hope back into the hopeless universe and life back into the dying realm. When we plant as God instructs even in the drought and despair of our lives, there will come a harvest and our empty arms with heavy hearts will become full with armloads of blessings filling our hearts again. No matter what we are going through, God challenges us to trust Him to plant right now, even in grief, anguish and despair...lay down seed, dig a hole of promise and pour yourself into it. Work the soil and water it with your tears, but do not let despair or grief become your grave. Plant. Feed. Water. Eventually you will harvest Joy as He will do it again! He will fill your arms with blessings and give you laughter once more. I remember the day we lost my brother tragically and how empty and despairing my parents were at that moment. It would've been very easy to walk away from God and ministry in particular as he was killed by another teen who attended our church. The people of the church split-some supportive of my family as their pastors were now deep in our grief and others were just flat hateful with harsh words of condemnation. Honestly, it was very hard at that moment to even think we would laugh again or even smile but years have passed. My brother's namesake, my son was born bringing joy again in my heart and I smile daily as I see my brother, whom he never met, in him all the time. The empty arms of my parents have been filled with the grandkids and more with those who were hurting and broken. My family understands grief and can embrace those who mourn deeper from a place of understanding. I don't understand why we have to walk through a place of grief but it doesn't have to be a place of despair because Jesus conquered death and the grave! Hold on for Joy is on its way.

Celebrate God all day, every day. I mean, revel in him! Make it as clear as you can to all you meet that you're on their side, working with them and not against them. Help them see that the Master is about to arrive. He could show up any minute!

Philippians 4:4-5

The Greatest Myth!

Last night as storms were rumbling, I stepped out and took this picture of the sky and thought that it looked like a bubble forming! You have to understand that there is this tongue in cheek myth of The Barksdale Bubble that we tease about around here always hoping it will be real and redirect bad weather away. It seems to happen quite a lot...weather breaks and goes around us forming a "bubble" on the radar, which is where the name comes from...although, as reporters have explained, that it's something to do with how close storms come to the radar and it cannot be read accurately...yada, yada, yada...the point is that it is a theory that some have, that Barksdale AFB has a weather machine that redirects weather in some manner. I don't rely on BAFB or a "bubble" as I have a God that I trust. As I stood there listening to the tornado close by us and watching this wall cloud, I thought again how amazing He is. I looked at the cloud then and thought how wonderful it would be if He just stepped out, that maybe that sound was Him rolling up the storm to step out and take us home. I kept waiting for the midnight cry, the trumpet call because I felt that overwhelming sense of time drawing to a close. This morning God spoke clearly to me that today is a day to celebrate life and Him all day through every circumstance. Today is a day to revel in His goodness and count my blessings but also to make sure that I share Him with all I meet. I will share His goodness and protection, I will share that I am for them just as He is for them whomever they might be. Most of all, I want all to know that Jesus could arrive any minute. This is a season of anticipating as children get excited about receiving gifts from Santa on Christmas Eve/morning but it is a great myth...bigger than the Elf on the Shelf or the Barksdale Bubble...more importantly because it should be the season of celebration in our hearts that Jesus came as a man to offer Himself as a spotless lamb for sacrifice to cover our multitude of sins. It should be a season of anticipation of His return for He is coming back to catch His bride away quickly. All the signs of His return are evident around us. What are we anticipating and celebrating? I mean, are we reveling in Him? Are we making it clear in all our actions and deeds, words and abilities in this season that Christ is the message of Christmas? The Message of Christ is where we get the word Christmas. If we are caught up in the flow of holiday functions, parties and elves without the central theme of Christ being the focus, we have missed it all. It is not about the baby in the manger; it is about the King of Glory who once came to save His people from their sins and is on His way to return and catch His bride away to be with Him forever. The greatest myth isn't Santa or the Barksdale Bubble. The greatest myth is that life can be lived without Christ. Jesus is coming and a life without Him is lost for eternity. Why wait? Be a myth buster and trust Him with your life. Be a myth buster and go tell others that Jesus is the one with the list checking it twice that matters, not Santa. Santa is a myth created to encourage children to behave, but Jesus isn't a myth. He's very real and He's coming very soon.

"I hear the sounds of the rushing mighty wind and it seems closer now than it has ever been...I can almost hear the trumpets as Gabriel sounds the call...at the midnight cry...we will be going home...as Jesus steps out on a cloud to take His children...the dead in Christ shall rise to meet Him in the air...then those that remain shall be quickly changed...at the midnight cry...we will be going home.

"'That's when Michael, the great angel-prince, champion of your people, will step in. It will be a time of trouble, the worst trouble the world has ever seen. But your people will be saved from the trouble, every last one found written in the Book. Many who have been long dead and buried will wake up, some to eternal life, others to eternal shame. "'Men and women who have lived wisely and well will shine brilliantly, like the cloudless, star-strewn night skies. And those who put others on the right path to life will glow like stars forever.

Daniel 12:1-3

Star Birth!

A star is born when atoms of light elements are squeezed under enough pressure for their nuclei to undergo fusion. In other words, star birth is a process of extreme trouble. Galaxies and nebulas change and are birthed, constantly set in motion by the unchanging hand of God. In Daniel, the arch angel visits Daniel to prophecy the future. He tells Daniel of the future after saying that he had been on his way to Daniel but gotten waylaid by another force. There is so much at play in our world every day that we do not see which is why scripture warns us that we are in a spiritual battlefield not one made of mankind alone. Star Wars fascinates us because it seems fantastical but in reality, there is more truth than fiction in the portrayal of forces beyond our control. "May the force be with you" doesn't work because the force is God himself and he is dependent on man. When I saw this incredible photo of how a star is formed, I was blown away. It is a mystery like that of the tiny cells coming together to form new life. We can understand it somewhat and even try to mimic it to an extent but the truth is that it is beyond our ability to fathom. We have an opportunity to have our name written in the Lamb's book of Life; Written in the red of His blood that sacrificed all for our sins so we can stand spotlessly before the throne of the Almighty Creator of all the galaxies and stars, representing Him and covered by His blood so that we are held to shine brilliantly for all eternity. Our role? Live for Him and shine for Him in this dark night leading others to the path of His forgiveness and mercy. He says that those who direct others to Him will glow like stars forever. Shame and remorse, regret and sorrow will be vast on that great day but they will pale beside the joy of the light of brilliance of those who lived wisely and shine brilliantly.

I love the look of the lights on homes this time of year. They sparkle through the night lighting up the area so others can see the beauty. The trees sparkle bringing a sense of beauty and hope, the night skies are clear and stars sparkle against the night canvas...all seems to be in waiting...He is coming again. He came once to save His people from sin now He comes to redeem them for all eternity. We shall behold Him. What kind of star will you be? An earth star shining for the moment in prideful success or an eternal star shining for the glory of God throughout eternity leading others to Him? Choose wisdom. Choose life. Choose to be a guiding light that will shine for all eternity through Him and with Him.

Don't waste your time on useless work, mere busywork, the barren pursuits of darkness. Expose these things for the sham they are. It's a scandal when people waste their lives on things they must do in the darkness where no one will see. Rip the cover off those frauds and see how attractive they look in the light of Christ. Wake up from your sleep, Climb out of your coffins; Christ will show you the light! So watch your step. Use your head. Make the most of every chance you get. These are desperate times!

Ephesians 5:11-16

Climb Out of the Coffin!

The beautiful flower in this portrait is a deadly nightshade called poison hemlock. It can kill you if ingested by touch, smell and certainly by taste but it is deceptive because it produces a beautiful flower, but even a small amount of hemlock on the skin causes severe rashes which can result in death if not treated. The flower is supposed to bring life and draw people to it, which it does, but it lures under false pretenses because even a tiny bit is poisonous. In this same manner, life and the pursuit of man's dreams can be barren, leaving one feeling lost and frustrated when all the labor comes to a head. Paul encourages us to expose the things for what they are and to step out of the grave life into true living. As my son graduates college today, I can truthfully say only about 1/4 of the classes he took had any value and in those classes, only a small percentage was actually something he will use. He had to waste a lot of time, effort and money to pursue a degree which he will not even be applying in his career because the degree wasn't about what he learned but about proving the point that he could achieve it by sticking through the morass. I am very proud of him because he made it but I am more proud because he kept himself true while he made it through. If you look at most of the pursuits of life in the light of Christ, it seems a waste, a sham, and an unattractive mess. We are called to climb out of the graves of this life and live a pursuit of Godliness. Live with our eyes on the prize of His glory and not personal gain. Watch your step and use your head as you climb out of that coffin of expectations of worldly gain and begin to walk in the freedom of Christ. Desperate times are here where you must make the most of every opportunity to live in Him.

Our days are filled with whirlwinds of activity, but which of these are truly of eternal value? Christ will show us the Light, the direction, the way if we pursue Him rather than our own agendas. It's a hard place to step out of what we have been shown or told is the path only to see that we were walking on a dark rutted path made by man instead of the oath of God's leading. When we begin to walk in His path, we still must watch our steps and use our head as there are always obstacles thrown straight at us but God tells us that He makes our paths straight and we can rejoice for the steps of a righteous man are ordered by God. Hemlock grows on wooded paths in shaded places where the sun cannot dry the poison out of the leaves. It hides in a dappled place so it can lure the unsuspecting into its clutches in times of desperation. Like poison ivy and sumac, these leafy lacy plants look beautiful but bring death. As we walk along the paths of life, there are many places to stop that look alluring, relaxing and attractive but they are really deadly nightshades that only look attractive in the dappled places of life. It is time to step into the path of full Sonshine where His truth shines on every place in our life. If we are walking on His path and in His light of truth, the falseness will show for what it is and be burned up in His glory. So many things we waste our lives in pursuit of when ultimately it is His glory we should be going after with all that is in us. Rip that covering off like the grads will rip those hats off today! Look forward to the brightness of what God has ahead of you. Do not get bogged down in the pursuit of man's ways or dreams but rather look to Him who is the author and finisher of our faith. Today is your chance and your opportunity to step out into His freedom and away from the weight of man's expectations.

He's got you and He's got this too!

My beloved friends, let us continue to love each other since love comes from God. Everyone who loves is born of God and experiences a relationship with God. The person who refuses to love doesn't know the first thing about God, because God is love—so you can't know him if you don't love. This is how God showed his love for us: God sent his only Son into the world so we might live through him. This is the kind of love we are talking about—not that we once upon a time loved God, but that he loved us and sent his Son as a sacrifice to clear away our sins and the damage they've done to our relationship with God.

1 John 4: 7-10

Sin Damaged!

I looked at my hands today and noticed the sunspots-the evidence of years of sun damage to my skin. Sure, I had spent years lying out in the sun perfecting my tan when I was young and yes, years more of carelessly going about my business without lotions to cover and protect but that didn't prepare me for the permanent damage to my once flawless skin. How can my hands look like my grandmother's hands used to look? The sun damage year after year without care has consequences that no amount of care after the fact can erase. The damage happened over the years and caught up to me...a gradual process of aging and the renewal process not being as good as it used to be. My friends, this is what happens to all of us when we allow the damage of sin to work itself on us. We damage our relationship with God by permissive small gestures of inattentive care. The day gets busy and the devotion gets missed. We hurry through the meal, skipping the prayer just once. We rush around the season to show after show, event after event until we are so exhausted and sick we cannot take time for Him. We get caught in the hustle and bustle of life until one day we realize that we failed to love Him and form a consistent relationship with Him. We allowed the indulgent lifestyle of busyness to take away the sacredness of relationship. We got caught up in our serving Him and forgot who He was. We were so caught up in the moments that we forgot who the moment was about. Love isn't a passive action but a choice activity that requires deliberate choice. God is love. His love is such that it makes an undeniable mark upon us, changing us forever, leaving us longing for a relationship with Him but often we get mixed up and allow the stage, the world, the serving and the celebration to become the moment rather than the love. I adore weddings & graduations with all the pomp and circumstance-the celebration, ceremony and excitement but it is so easy to get caught up in the excitement of the ceremonies and celebrations that we forget who they are about until suddenly it is over.

We must confess that the sin damage has caught up with us. Those days of lying out in the world not taking care of our relationship with Him, just simply soaking up the ways of the world around us carelessly never thinking of the results in later years. The tanning beds of places we shouldn't have popped into now echo on our spiritual robes with a yellow hue of age rather than the purity of white. The rushed moments of skipping prayer and devotional now show as those frayed spots of sin damage on our soul when we rush into the next seasonal activity without a care that this moment, this holy moment may be the one...the one that could change our history. That one moment we skipped the time with Him could be the moment He whispered the exact words of peace we needed as we anxiously hurried into the place of service. This is what we are talking about...not a once upon a time, wish upon a star, but a constant, sacrificial love that perfects time instead of demanding it. The person who refuses to love doesn't know God because you cannot know God, who is Love, if you don't know love. Love spots are easy to see. They show up as easily as spots on a leopard because they are evident in word and deed. They don't come from carelessly lying about being loved on by others but rather are genetically reborn with the relationship with Christ. The love begins to pour through the cells so that it is fragrant and rich, obvious to all who encounter the person who they are connected to as they demonstrate the family traits. The traits of love, kindness, gentleness, meekness and self control cover their gait and their mannerisms. They walk in love, act in love, talk in love and exude love to all they meet. They don't have to wait for age spots to show up because the love spots show up first and cover those aged sin spots with the precious blood of Jesus. He washes those careless moments spent in untoward places and whitens that gown so it shines as pure as freshly fallen snow. God sent His son to clear away the sin damage by covering us in love spots. As we live through Him, these love spots grow connecting us to who He is so that the love overflows. We are so blessed that His love covers our aging ways and although this body may lay claim to lots of sun damage, it's the Son repair that we can lay claim to in eternity. Sin damage is washed away with the covering of His lotion of love. Bought, packaged and delivered....it's up to Him to apply the lotion of salvation and forgiveness to our sin damaged souls.

I think it's time to go bask in the Son's love and rest my weary soul.

The people who walked in darkness have seen a great light. For those who lived in a land of deep shadows— light! sunbursts of light! You repopulated the nation, you expanded its joy. Oh, they're so glad in your presence! Festival joy! The joy of a great celebration, sharing rich gifts and warm greetings. The abuse of oppressors and cruelty of tyrants— all their whips and clubs and curses— Is gone, done away with, a deliverance as surprising and sudden as Gideon's old victory over Midian. The boots of all those invading troops, along with their shirts soaked with innocent blood, Will be piled in a heap and burned, a fire that will burn for days! For a child has been born—for us! the gift of a son—for us! He'll take over the running of the world. His names will be: Amazing Counselor, Strong God, Eternal Father, Prince of Wholeness. His ruling authority will grow, and there'll be no limits to the wholeness he brings. He'll rule from the historic David throne over that promised kingdom. He'll put that kingdom on a firm footing and keep it going With fair dealing and right living, beginning now and lasting always. The zeal of God-of-the-Angel-Armies will do all this.
Isaiah 9:2-7

Son-burst Light!

When I saw this cloud in the sky, it looked to me exactly like an angel about to proclaim the coming of Jesus! My heart tripled in beat and then the rain started. The blue turned to gray skies and the cold wet misery stole my joy because I didn't hold onto it. The joy of that moment should last forever but somehow I let it go when the shadows started creeping in. It is much easier to celebrate a light and look forward with hope when you have been in darkness than to celebrate the light when it grows dim as darkness creeps in. Those who have lived in a land of great shadows marvel at light and celebrate in wonderment but those who have held the light begin to wonder what the big deal is and lose sight of the Sonburst. Being glad in God's presence shouldn't be a momentary thing that fades when His glorious presence is shadowed by the things around us that set us back. That is when our eyes should look even more towards the light of His love and celebrate that we know where He is, who He is and what He is about but somehow we forget that we had the light the whole time. The joy of a celebration and sharing gifts and warm greetings is there because we know who is bringing the light. The names of Christ Jesus in the roles He plays-Amazing Counselor, Strong & Mighty God, Eternal Father, Prince of Peace & Wholeness are only part of the infinite names and roles He plays in our lives but we get so caught up putting Him into the boxes of our lives that we forget that Light cannot be held or bound by darkness. It is the antitheses of darkness-the repelling and replacement of the same. Light projects far into the nether reaches calling to those lost and yet it remains consistent in the place it started. The giving of light into darkness doesn't dim the light nor extinguish it but rather makes the miracle of it more evident. Walking outside with a flashlight that is on is the same in day or night but in daytime, the flashlight is rather ignored because the sun-light outshines it and the light from the flashlight is much more evident in darkness. The light didn't change. The location didn't change. The change was the attitude or light surround. Your light and your joy in Jesus should remain constant so that when you are walking in the daylight of life celebration, people can see your light on but focus on the light around you, and when you are walking in hard times, the darkness doesn't pierce you but rather allows that light to draw others. Your light of life isn't determined by your circumstances but rather whether you have the light on. The cloud was still there when the rain started. The light was still there. The difference was my perception. Sonburst light in your life is always there as He is always there. You may choose to look around you at all the other lights in times of joy and fail to realize that He is there but He is constant. There are no limits to the wholeness and peace He brings. He is always light. The rain and cold are still here but so is the light. It is all about personal perspective. Are you looking at the light and walking in the light or are you looking at the darkness while walking in the light? You choose-He left the light on for eternity.

Jesus sent his twelve harvest hands out with this charge: "Don't begin by traveling to some far-off place to convert unbelievers. And don't try to be dramatic by tackling some public enemy. Go to the lost, confused people right here in the neighborhood. Tell them that the kingdom is here. Bring health to the sick. Raise the dead. Touch the untouchables. Kick out the demons. You have been treated generously, so live generously.

Matthew 10: 5-8

Tackle Your Yard!

It is always easier to see the flaw at a distance than to see the one up close. I am not a perfectionist by nature but I do hold myself to a high level of accountability and sometimes that causes extreme anxiety as it is hard to manage the expectations. When Jesus was calling men to follow Him, He did not call the chosen. He chose the called. He went into places where He saw men/women working in their marketplace and he called them to follow Him. Their workplace became their marketplace of ministry and He chose them from that calling. They weren't the upper crust or those that were of means who had time to devote to His service but rather those who were dependent on their marketplace to live. He knew they would follow Him and would work in the place of service not expecting it to be handed to them because they were workers. He told them not to plan to travel afar off converting unbelievers but to go to the lost in their own backyard and tell them of Him. He said to touch the untouchable and bring health to the sick. In other words, go to your marketplace of ministry and get to work. He tells us to live generously as we have been treated and kick out the demons. It's not as dramatic as tackling a public enemy but rather starting in your own yard. We tend to like to think on bigger terms than starting with our own place but the truth is that the best place to start is in our own yard. Tackling the dirty jobs means taking care of the mess we make first hand, then stretching out to those closest to us before thinking we can go further than our own area. It's a step by step process. So many times we get overwhelmed looking at the mass of expectation rather than realizing that it is simply one step at a time beginning in our own yard. Start small. This is what Jesus was saying. Don't try to go big and convert people from afar when you haven't done the work in your own area. Start by blessing your neighbors, your coworkers, your friends and demonstrate the love of God there first. Believe me, if you cannot demonstrate God's love to your own family in your words, actions and deeds then your ministry is going to be ineffective anyway. Quit trying to be more than enough and try to be all you can for those in your life. Don't think you have to change the entire world when you haven't yet made the change to those closest to you. Start there. What does your yard look like? Can you blow the leaves from Your yard and do your neighbors too? Can you take the time to be more to your spouse in kind words, deeds and patience with their needs? Are you stretching yourself thin, blessing others but losing patience with your family and snapping at them? Tackle your yard first. Clean up Your attitude and your behavior with your own family then you can share the truth with others. Sure, it is much easier to preach it than to live it but if you cannot live it then who is going to believe it when you say it. Your actions speak louder than your words to all in your path.

What are your actions saying about Jesus?

Jesus said these things.
Then, raising his eyes in prayer, he said:
Father, it's time.
Display the bright splendor of your Son
So the Son in turn may show your bright splendor.
You put him in charge of everything human
So he might give real and eternal life to all in his care.
And this is the real and eternal life:
That they know you,
The one and only true God,
And Jesus Christ, whom you sent.
I glorified you on earth
By completing down to the last detail
What you assigned me to do.
And now, Father,
glorify me with your very own splendor,
The very splendor I had in your presence
Before there was a world.

John 17: 1-5

The Splendor Before…!

Before there is ice, there is water and before water there is hydrogen and oxygen and before these two elements combine, there is air. When I look at the splendor of a waterfall, I only see the incredible mass of water falling, I do not see the before usually. Before that water droplet fell in splendor catching the rays of the sun and reflection of rainbow light, what was it doing? How was it positioned? Was it carried along or was it carrying? Was it air that became heavy with hydrogen and changed forms into rain that fell to the earth then ran down the mountainside? Each droplet of water has a story of importance and yet I will never know it, but the Father does. As Jesus waged a battle in The Garden and went through the crucifixion of sacrifice, he was waiting to transfigure back to Heaven. He prayed a prayer over us. He knew the time had come for a small vision of His splendor to be revealed. He knew this before. He experienced life like no other and He stood ready to accept His splendor again as a King of Glory, as only He had known before…and He prayed for us. He knew the journey He would take over the next few days. He knew it would be gruesome, full of doubt by all and scary, but He knew the Before. John says it is impossible to write down all that happened and all that Jesus did in His time on Earth because it would fill tomes of books but he was writing the important highlights down. The journey of the baby from the manger wasn't told in John as he only told the ministry highlights. John doesn't tell the story of the water droplet but of The Word. He tells the developing story of the Waterfall-the power, the dimension, the Life, The Light. He tells the story of the splendor but not the splendor before…only Jesus prays that in His prayer. Jesus says, Display the bright splendor of your Son so the Son can in turn show your bright splendor. He who knew the before prayed that we might see the glory so we could understand the before and yet so many miss it. It isn't about the star, the manger, the baby….it is about the cross. The splendor before…before the sin. The splendor before…before the created. The splendor before…the bright splendor…of God Himself was displayed on a cross of man's making and yet we missed it. His splendor of glory looks nothing like we anticipated so we turned away not realizing the transcendence of that moment. The splendor before…the glory of God on display…Love in its purest form that God himself would take on the form of man and suffer to the point of death on the cross to display His splendor of glory to us. The water turned to wine. The wine turned to blood. The blood turned to glory. The glory turned to love.

The love shed as a tear caught in the hand of God….His splendor so revealed on a cross of love.

The Word was first,
the Word present to God,
God present to the Word.
The Word was God,
in readiness for God from day one.

The Word became flesh and blood,
and moved into the neighborhood.
We saw the glory with our own eyes,
the one-of-a-kind glory,
like Father, like Son,
Generous inside and out,
true from start to finish.

John 1: 1-2, 14

True Form!

Shopping and trying to find clothing is difficult because sizes vary so much. I ordered an XL jacket and it looks like it might fit a toddler. The truth is that standards aren't the same across the world or even across families. What one person thinks is ok, another feels wronged. What one person thinks is overdoing, another feels like it is nothing, lazy or a pitiful attempt. The Word was the first and only true form establishing a standard. The Word is God, is from God, is present to God and is in God. Jesus is The Word. God spoken, God breathed, readiness for God. When Jesus came and dwelt among men, it was the glory of God coming to earth before our own eyes, filling the true form of who God is, the standard previously never met, suddenly fulfilled. I remember going with my daughter-in-law to look at wedding dresses and try them on. None fit, but the one she chose was the right one for her from the start. Then it had to be altered through many fittings. I remember when it was finally ready to wear as she put it on in breathless anticipation with the shoes and looked into the mirror as she realized it finally fit. It was like a final moment of recognition had happened. God calls His bride to come up to His standard and only in the moment of all the fittings and altering through His word do we fulfill His glory. His glory is a standard of performance, perfection and fulfillment to achieve. We will go through fittings and developing in our life where the skin we are in doesn't appear to fit. We will go through times of incredible loss and amazing gains. We will go through great moments, sad occurrences and tragedies but all through it we must look forward to the purpose of His glory. The dress she wore was purposed to make her shine in the moment of revealing herself to her bridegroom as a bride worthy of him.

There was no doubt when I looked at my son's face that she had accomplished her purpose encasing herself in a gown to showcase her glory. God has called us as His bride to prepare for His glory. He has called us to wear a garment of His glory for presentation because this garment of love is His word and it stands in His glory outshining everything in and of Earth. When anything comes at you, if you stand in the glory of His word, then the battle will be already won. The gown, stronger than teflon as anything that comes at it will fail. Jesus Himself used the word in the great temptation. Everything that was thrown at Him was answered with, "it is written…". This is our crowning glory that we come under The Word in readiness for God from day one! The perfect form-the true standard-the one of a kind-one size fits all-The true form-The word.

Why would you ever complain, O Jacob,
or, whine, Israel, saying,
"God has lost track of me.
He doesn't care what happens to me"?
Don't you know anything? Haven't you been listening?
God doesn't come and go. God lasts.
He's Creator of all you can see or imagine.
He doesn't get tired out,
doesn't pause to catch his breath.
And he knows everything, inside and out.
He energizes those who get tired,
gives fresh strength to dropouts.
For even young people tire and drop out,
young folk in their prime stumble and fall.
But those who wait upon God get fresh strength.
They spread their wings and soar like eagles,
They run and don't get tired,
they walk and don't lag behind.

Isaiah 40: 27-31

God Lasts!

The cold set into my bones as I realized that the power was out and my electric blanket had turned off. Things fail and break at unexpected times. People fail and fall apart but God doesn't fail. We often attribute our abilities or lack thereof to God but He doesn't come/go...He's better than an Energizer Bunny because He lasts beyond the expected and the unexpected. Isaiah says He is Creator of all you can think or imagine and He never tires nor does He need to pause to catch His breath. As my husband goes in and out of this cold trying to repair the generator and figure out what is going on, I am reminded of a God who is constantly in charge, working behind the scenes to make things work for our good. We are like little babies without His mastery of all things. We are lost and without ability, without His magnificent tolerance of our ways and our whininess. We whine and complain that things don't go our way when we should instead be counting our blessings, for God hasn't lost track of us, nor has He quit caring. He is constant and ever working on our behalf even while we are content though often we fail to measure it. God provides us energy when we are fatigued; filling us with His fresh strength that has no fuel shortage or battery limit. He knows our ins and outs, comings and goings and more. He knows everything down to the tiniest details. His strength isn't tasked or overwhelmed like a power grid nor does He lose patience or run out of oil.

He is constant. He is a present source in time of trouble. He is ever working on our behalf before we think to ask. Our God is an awesome God. No cold storm can outdo Him nor any unexpected power surges or lack. He isn't dependent on man's abilities nor man's supply sources. He is God. Wait on Him. He will renew us so that we once again spread our wings and soar as eagles. Wait on God. His timing is perfect.

He doesn't lag behind but knows the time and place. Wait on Him.

While he was trying to figure a way out, he had a dream. God's angel spoke in the dream: "Joseph, son of David, don't hesitate to get married. Mary's pregnancy is Spirit-conceived. God's Holy Spirit has made her pregnant. She will bring a son to birth, and when she does, you, Joseph, will name him Jesus—'God saves'—because he will save his people from their sins." This would bring the prophet's embryonic revelation to full term: Watch for this—a virgin will get pregnant and bear a son;
They will name him Immanuel
(Hebrew for "God is with us").

Matthew 1: 20-23

The Way Thru!

While he was trying to figure a way out....God saved. While we were yet sinners...Christ died for us! While we are in our situations, God has already made a way thru. God isn't a God of limitations but one of possibilities. We sometimes see only the limitations when He has already worked the impossible that we do not yet see. We as humans are always trying to figure a way out of our unfortunate circumstances but what if we could instead look at them as a parting of waters...a way thru rather than a way out. The Israelites got to a place where there was no solution ahead so they turned their hearts back to slavery and death trying to figure a way out rather than looking to the God of the impossible who had just brought them out of an impossible situation thru miraculous circumstances. What does it take for God to get through our hard heads? God's will is imminent over all things but we have a choice to fight or yield. We get so set in our way or the highway that we fail to recognize the miracle in front of us that is in the making. I will admit that many times my heart has gotten broken when circumstances didn't go the way we thought they should. Our impossibilities are only potential for God. Joseph had an angel speak to him in a dream but he had to be willing to listen or he would've missed out on being a part of the greatest story ever told. Joseph got to name Him, Jesus....Jesus-God Saves, Immanuel-God is with us. Each time we celebrate the season of His birth, it is an opportunity to realize that we are celebrating the way thru our impossibilities. There are almost 1000 names God is called by in scripture and yet we still doubt the possibilities in our circumstances.

We have seen time after time when God has moved and made ways when there seemed to be no way-both in scriptures and in our lives but yet we still get stuck at the Red Sea of our lives and want to turn back, giving up the ground He has given us. We must learn from all the examples that God isn't a God of limits but a God of impossibilities! We must begin to look at the circumstances before us as potential rather than as walls or oceans stopping us. We must begin to embrace Who He Is rather than what our limitations want to box Him into. He is bigger than that ocean; in fact, He spoke that ocean into being and at His command it moves. Life marches on whether you want it to or not, but you have the choice to accept the God of the impossible who is making a way thru or to stay in your mental box of unrest, unhappiness and imposing circumstances. God is moving across the land. You can choose to see His power and be a part or to mentally stay in slavery to that thing that keeps you beat down mentally and powerless. Joseph chose to believe the angel and he had an amazing life of impossible circumstances becoming possible. He had to choose to see the way thru in God's eyes and not in circumstances that looked bleak. God could've used another but He chose Mary & Joseph. Time to make a choice. Will you take hold of the Master's hand, this God of 1000 names and impossibilities being potential or will you hold onto your frustrations and depression of the limited mindset? It is your choice: The God of the Impossible or the god of this world with its fragility and limits. God will make a way where there seems to be no way. I've seen Him do it thousands of times. That ocean...about to roll back to dry ground...that mountain is about to move, that impossible circumstance...a miracle in the making.

The people who walked in darkness
have seen a great light.
For those who lived in a land of deep shadows—
light! sunbursts of light!
You repopulated the nation,
you expanded its joy.
Oh, they're so glad in your presence!
Festival joy!
The joy of a great celebration,
sharing rich gifts and warm greetings.
The abuse of oppressors and cruelty of tyrants—
all their whips and clubs and curses—
Is gone, done away with, a deliverance
as surprising and sudden as Gideon's old victory over Midian.
The boots of all those invading troops,
along with their shirts soaked with innocent blood,
Will be piled in a heap and burned,
a fire that will burn for days!
For a child has been born—for us!
the gift of a son—for us!
He'll take over
the running of the world.
His names will be: Amazing Counselor,
Strong God,
Eternal Father,
Prince of Wholeness.
His ruling authority will grow,
and there'll be no limits to the wholeness he brings.
He'll rule from the historic David throne
over that promised kingdom.
He'll put that kingdom on a firm footing
and keep it going
With fair dealing and right living,
beginning now and lasting always.
The zeal of God-of-the-Angel-Armies
will do all this.

Isaiah 9: 2-7

A Great Light!

I must admit that there is little that makes a momma's heart happier than having her babies back at home. When we first found out we were to have a child, the joy was palpable but then the sorrow came when we lost our first child...introducing fear into the next pregnancy as I immediately started having issues. Thankfully the doctor figured out it was Rh factor and soon we we're welcoming our firstborn son. Oh the delight and joy of great celebration and when Christmas came, we pulled out all the stops of festivities traveling to all the families homes to share our joy! I cannot imagine the joy of Jesus' birth being any more than ours but it is because His birth wasn't just for His family or His line or heritage but it was for deliverance of His people and all those afar off even unto the ends of the Earth. When you are walking in a shadowed place, the cold and dark seep into your bones causing fear and frustration. But God sent His son that we might have light-not weights...not darkness...not pain...not fear...not panic...not disappointment, nor discomfort, nor discouragement, nor failure...Life...He came in the form of a baby to share His light in the way we understand it...as a baby. He took on the form of a tiny embryo to help us understand the importance of LIFE! This strong God, eternal Father, Amazing Counselor and Prince of Wholeness & Peace took on the form of a baby in the lowest of circumstances to show us His light.

The circumstances of His birth were miraculous and awful at the same time. This gift of life brought about the sacrifice which signaled an end to slavery to sin. This gift brought change on a mighty scale but those parents while knowing the mighty load of raising the Messiah were consumed like all of us with the everyday tasks of paying taxes and traveling late in pregnancy, no room in an inn, birth in a stable, etc. while also having to change everything in their life because of the birth of a son. When we found out we were expecting our second child, it was such a shock because we had been told we may not have any others due to the difficulties of the first birth and the RH factor. Gabriel was born less than two years after John and immediately they bonded and our hearts were full to overflowing. I look at them today reveling in life and think of all the joys they have brought me. As we travel once again bringing our best to gather together with our families, my heart knows time is changing and the opportunities to be together are slimmer and less often. As I reflect on the birth and death of my Savior, I reflect as a mother on that young man, the Son of God, raised by a young mother who knew He was God and yet He was her baby. I just imagine the pride and joy she had at His birth and the fear and frustration that so easily takes hold...there she held the Prince of Peace in her arms and the zeal of all the Angel armies. The purpose of all mankind and the redemption of all people, wrapped in swaddling clothes as the perfect lamb of God lying in a sacrificial repose in a manger. The Great Light of the Bethlehem star bringing strangers in to see this Messiah...what joy!

Warm greetings to all on this Christmas!

God can pour on the blessings in astonishing ways so that you're ready for anything and everything, more than just ready to do what needs to be done. As one psalmist puts it, He throws caution to the winds, giving to the needy in reckless abandon. His right-living, right-giving ways never run out, never wear out. This most generous God who gives seed to the farmer that becomes bread for your meals is more than extravagant with you. He gives you something you can then give away, which grows into full-formed lives, robust in God, wealthy in every way, so that you can be generous in every way, producing with us great praise to God.

2 Corinthians 9: 8-11

Contemplated Seed!

Today I have been thinking deeply about blessing and what it means. In 2 Corinthians, Paul says God CAN pour on blessings in astonishing ways so you are ready for anything and everything, more than just ready for what needs to be done. It goes on to say that this most generous God who gives seed to the farmer that becomes bread for your meals is more than extravagant with us. He gives us something to be sowed, given away and grown into fully formed lives that are robust in God and wealthy in every way so we can be generous and produce great praises to God. I think of the story of the little red hen who worked so hard at each stage of her life to produce the bread but no one wanted to be a part of it. They didn't want to do the work nor put in the effort it took to achieve the blessings...they were only about receiving. Now, let's go back to the CAN. It doesn't say God will. It says God CAN as in God is able to, willing to, wants to but there is an action we must take. We must be like a river and not a dam. We must be a flow through not a stopping point. We must be willing to give generously, love generously and be generous in our actions, words and deeds to others. Selfish mindset stops the blessings of God because we are not ready for anything and everything, more than just ready to do what needs to be done. I think of this as an employer. I have several employees who go the extra mile with whatever I give them and it is to those I first turn to give extra towards because I know it will be used to benefit all of us and our clients. There are others who are dams and no matter what is given to them, they shut it down and go no further. God sees our hearts and knows our intents. He sees our actions, words and deeds. His right-living, right-giving ways never run out nor wear out and He wants to give to us in reckless abandon but He expects you to do with what you have first. Self-indulgence and being consumed with me, mine, my feelings and my life only end up in a selfish-attitude driven life which stops the current of God's blessings in your life. There is a story that Jesus tells in Matthew 25:14 and Luke 19:11 of the 3 men with money given to them by their boss. The one who was given the most went out and doubled it by investing into the lives of others...a risk with rewards. The second also doubled the money but the third hid it because he was afraid, so he lost out in the end. God gives us each a measure of faith and blessings. How we use them, accrue them, and share them matters. If we hide them or use them up on ourselves, that is all we will have is that measure here on Earth. If we invest into His kingdom with all the risks involved, He will pour out double portions.

We must take a look at what we are doing with the blessings that God has given us. Are we investing into His ways, His faithfulness, His kingdom or are we investing in our own selves, heaping rewards upon ourselves and loving ourselves more than others. Think life is tough? We need to look around us at others who are in greater need and begin to invest in them from our meager blessings then watch the storehouse of God's blessings begin to flow. Have we Invested a little then nothing happened...well, we must check the attitude of our heart. Do we invest into the lives of others with selfish purpose? Are we spitting into the wind all of the vileness of regrets? Are we living or loving? Is our tongue or words being what they should? Are we lifting up or tearing down? Are we building for the future of God's kingdom or are we stockpiling for ourselves? What are we planting? Nurturing in others? growing? Investing? God is able and He is willing...the faith is the trigger. Have a little and need a lot? The psalmist says God throws caution to the wind giving to the needy in reckless abandon. Perhaps it is time to be like the widow with only a little who gave all she had only to be blessed with abundance. Instead of bemoaning what we don't have and how terrible everything is, perhaps change to counting those blessings. I know that God sees and when we invest faithfully into His kingdom, He supplies all our needs according to His riches in Heaven. He goes above and beyond. He is better than our fathers and mothers, sisters and brothers. He gave His own son for sacrifice for our sins and there is nothing that He won't do for us if we invest in Him. We need to look around at the opportunities for investment and watch what God will do. We cannot just sit on it, contemplate it, think about it, hide it...the release of the blessings comes from the investment of the seed. Find your seed blessing and invest it then nurture it, water it, grow it through faithfulness, fertilize it with His love and prayers...then watch it multiply into harvest. Jesus doesn't fail.

Whenever, though, they turn to face God as Moses did, God removes the veil and there they are—face-to-face! They suddenly recognize that God is a living, personal presence, not a piece of chiseled stone. And when God is personally present, a living Spirit, that old, constricting legislation is recognized as obsolete. We're free of it! All of us! Nothing between us and God, our faces shining with the brightness of his face. And so we are transfigured much like the Messiah, our lives gradually becoming brighter and more beautiful as God enters our lives and we become like him.

2 Corinthians 3: 16-18

Transfigured!

The skyline is transformed into something much more beautiful than it normally is....much like a painting by an artist renowned. I've heard red in the morning is a sailor's warning but the beauty of it is astounding...as the morning light creeps in, it fades to pink and hues of pastels with bright light breaking through. One of my dearest friends took his final journey after a long battle with cancer but cancer didn't win. It is almost as if he became lighter and brighter, winging his way to his Heavenly home transfigured by his love for God until his ethereal presence could no longer inhabit that mortal frame. God removed the veil and welcomed him home. Paul in this letter to the Corinthians describes the relationship with God as a turning to face God so we recognize that God is a living, personal presence not a series of rules set in stone. God is personally present as a living Spirit indwelling us and the more we seek Him, the more we become transformed into light and beauty drawing others to Him. There is nothing between us and God. Our faces shine with His brightness when we behold His presence face to face...that light is visible to others who recognize it for what it is and it draws those who do not. It is impossible to walk in great darkness when one has seen the light because your eyes will track towards the light just as your heart will. The only way to not be drawn by the light is to deliberately turn in the opposite direction so you cannot see the light and even then you know it is there drawing you. I think of so many I know who have turned back towards darkness, embracing that bitter place because the light dimmed or flickered in their lives when they experienced a hardship, a loss or a disappointment so deeply that they had prayed and believed would have a different outcome. The purpose of the Spirit is to pray in the will of The Father when our spirit doesn't know how to pray. Our spirit is weak and easily disconnected, discouraged and distracted by things of this world but His Spirit knows no discouragement nor distractions because it is one with Him-the veil removed, intimately connected. When God passed by Moses on the mountaintop, His presence surrounded Moses so much that as he came down the people covered him with a veil because they couldn't see him as he was transfigured in form. He took the veil off when he spoke with God to have nothing between them. Grab this significance. The veil or covering of the head, face is a separation from the norm. It is a covering between God and man which many religions still use symbolically or even as a requirement to lessen status. God told Moses to construct a veil or curtain to separate the Holy of Holies-the place God dwelt-from the regular part of the church when construction was done and only the High Priest could enter there to receive God's words and instructions. It was such that they put a bell with a rope on the ankle of the priest so that if he failed to be pure or please God and he died, they could pull him out if the bell quit sounding.

But...Jesus was crucified for our sin becoming the ultimate sacrificial lamb that was spotless and His sacrifice ended these rules-when He gave up His spirit into God's hands, the veil in the Holy of Holies ripped in two and the sky rolled back. Think of it-in that moment, God himself removed all the rules of old that separated Him from man, becoming a man himself and giving that life for our atonement. That is amazing love! That is artistry beyond the highest. That is beyond mortal comprehension that a King of glory would come down and offer Himself as a sacrifice to remove the separation between Himself and those He loved. He didn't change His mind and undo...He broke the back of the burden of law and became the fulfillment of that law in order to free us from the burden. Now, we can turn directly to God with our burdens and no longer have to go through others. He put men/women on equal footing. Masters and slaves are equal in His eyes. No one-not a preacher nor a saint has a higher status. One cannot promote oneself nor demote. There are no places of status with God. The one who turns to Him and fully embraces the Light sees all He is just as the one who has walked in the Light their whole life. So why walk in darkness when you can walk in light? Why carry a burden of rules, laws and trying to do right when you can give your burdens to Him and walk lightly? Sin has no hold on you when you walk in the Light. Darkness can surround you but if you walk in the Light, it has no grasp on you. It is in the turning or stepping out of the Light where the burdens once again pile on and become troublesome so that one looks back and in turning away from the Light sees a false light and becomes confused. When God has entered your life, it is as if you become more beautiful and brighter as we become more like Him surrounded by His light-transfigured by Him.

When my soul is in the dumps, I rehearse
everything I know of you,
From Jordan depths to Hermon heights,
including Mount Mizar.
Chaos calls to chaos,
to the tune of whitewater rapids.
Your breaking surf, your thundering
breakers crash and crush me.
Then God promises to love me all day,
sing songs all through the night!
My life is God's prayer.

Why are you down in the dumps, dear soul?
Why are you crying the blues?
Fix my eyes on God—
soon I'll be praising again.
He puts a smile on my face.
He's my God.

Psalms 42: 6-8, 11

Surfing Promises!

Overwhelming waves of grief, unimaginable storms of pain and breaking whitewater rapids of despair surrounded David as he wrote these words. He was in complete despair and yet, he knew the answer wasn't in the disappointment but rather in the promises. He began to recount what he knew of God from the beginning of time. He realized that the love of God was the breaking surf of thundering breakers that crashed and crushed but yet restored life. If we remember that God is our God and we fix our eyes on Him, then we will find that praising Him puts a smile on our faces. Discouraging times come but His love prevails and when we focus on the promises and not on the circumstances, our joy is renewed rather than snuffed out. Like thunderstorms with lightning comes and brings the necessary rain to water the crops, life's storms come with hidden blessings if we but look.

When we focus our eyes on the King of Glory and hold to His promises despite the situations we are in, the love of God grows in us fed and watered by the faith in His promises. The storms may rage and the lightning may strike causing fear and even hurting but the blessings become the growth of the future when the promises of God are held onto strongly despite what is seen, felt, and heard.

Trauma, pain and grief come breaking against the Rock of His promises but the promises are unchanged for His foundation is strong, unwieldy and lasting. Today, I celebrated the life of a man of God with his loving family, realizing that God's promises sing songs to all of us through His love all day long. Our lives are God's prayer and when we focus on the truth of His promises, praise stays on our lips!

Let me give you some good advice; I'm looking you in the eye and giving it to you straight: "Don't be ornery like a horse or mule that needs bit and bridle to stay on track." God-defiers are always in trouble; God-affirmers find themselves loved every time they turn around. Celebrate God. Sing together—everyone! All you honest hearts, raise the roof!
Psalms 32:8-11

God Luck!

A lucky penny, a stress stone, a lucky charm or a sensory relaxer all have the same thing in common: to bring calm hope. David, the psalmist says in his sage advice that we can choose to be a God affirmer holding to His promises reveling in His love or a God defier held to the track of God ways by bit and bridle like an ornery horse or mule. In other words, God's will shall be done as He said regardless, for He is God but we can be loved and celebrated as we celebrate Him or we can be held onto the right track through sheer determination and prayer by those who love us.

"Count yourself lucky, how happy you must be— you get a fresh start, your slate is wiped clean. Count yourself lucky— God holds nothing against you and you're holding nothing back from him. When I kept it all inside, my bones turned to powder, my words became daylong groans. The pressure never let up; all the juices of my life dried up. Then I let it all out; I said, "I'll come clean about my failures to God." Suddenly the pressure was gone— my guilt dissolved, my sin disappeared. These things add up. Every one of us needs to pray; when all hell breaks loose and the dam bursts we'll be on high ground, untouched. God's my island hideaway, keeps danger far from the shore, throws garlands of hosannas around my neck." Psalms 32:1-7 MSG

David's advice comes from a place of knowing. He tried the road of hard headedness, going his own way, making poor choices and having the bridle of life's failures steer him back to the path of forgiveness and mercy. He knows as he writes this song that fighting against God and waging battle with God are the opposite sides of the same coin because God is God and we are His. God Himself knows us but like a parent He loves us and allows us to discover the challenges of life through the hard or the easy. I was always fascinated by the people who refused to follow directions and chose to do things their own way. My thought was, pause to read the instructions to follow and it is so much easier but sometimes we just want our own way. Recently, we had a family conversation about the importance of others in the path of the Christian walk. Is the community of God and church attendance truly important? Much like those who refuse to receive instructions and would like to just do it their way, many choose to walk it out themselves without the constant support of the family of God. They see the church as a weight holding them to standards set by others rather than an anchor of support. Each boat of life sails on a troubled sea no matter what it looks like to others on social media. We all have trials and tribulations. The choice to anchor in Jesus and be surrounded by other ships who also anchor in Him is the choice of attending a church and joining with other believers. A ship alone at sea without an anchor in a storm is knocked off track at best and overwhelmed easily by the storms. The ship who anchors in Jesus can weather the storms of life but those that anchor together are a supportive system to one another supplying and steering when one alone can get a little stressed or strained. God tells us in His word to not neglect the assembly of the brethren for a reason.

The network of believers holds and anchors us to the place of power, hope, sound mind and strength. It reminds us in times of trouble and encourages us in times of storms that we are not alone. When we cannot see the anchor nor feel it, we can look at those around us and know the anchor holds. God luck isn't a chance like rolling a dice but rather a formula of truth. We can either hold to His unchanging hand in uncharted waters of life or we can drift through on our own hoping we make it by sheer luck, blown by the winds of life, battered by the storms and overwhelmed by the endless waiting in life. It is a choice. God luck isn't really luck at all but good advice. It is the choice to hold to the love and promises in His word or stay the course no matter how it looks. In the eye of the storm is the quiet and rest where we can stay if we trust in Him. He alone is our anchor but the ships around us can remind us and support us in the eye if we choose to look to them and be a part of the network of believers. It is a choice....but it is also how God luck is made!

"If only my words were written in a book–better yet, chiseled in stone! Still, I know that God lives– the One who gives me back my life–and eventually he'll take his stand on earth.And I'll see him– even though I get skinned alive!– see God myself, with my very own eyes. Oh, how I long for that day!

Job 19: 23-27

Chiseled in Stone!

As the drawing down of this year closes and the dawn of a new year comes, I see people choosing scriptures to be guided by daily for the year or words for the year, setting goals, resolutions and dreaming of what can be from what was not. Job was a man who was God locked and loaded. God knew no matter what that Job would stand because He knew that greater is He Himself than the tempter. Job had walked an arduous journey of life... losing all he had including his children, friends and even his wife had turned on him. Job held onto the fact that He knew God lived and even though Job got everything he listed paid back in full (although I do not think losing a child or family can ever be paid back in full), Job longed for That Day! The day he longed for has come for Job and for some of our loved ones this year...the day we will see Him-God Himself, with our own eyes. If only, is a phrase of regret and yet one of promise should you choose. I know for a fact that many of us had "if only" moments this year. If only I had, if only she/he had, if only this or that....these are all areas or moments of regret that we look back on with nostalgic desire for change and we set goals to be better, make better choices, and anchor ourselves deeper. We plan and post. We strive and hope. I, like Job, say I know that God lives and soon He will take His stand on Earth. Whether I see Him with my own eyes in Heaven or on Earth, I will see Him soon. My longing for That Day is my eternal hope. We should live our lives as if today is That Day! I have a friend who closes his radio broadcast every night by asking, "If today was your last day, who would you call? What would you say? Why are you waiting? Make that call!" I agree. As this year closes, Who would you like to take to Heaven with you? What would you say to them if you knew today was your or their last day on Earth? Why are you waiting because Jesus is coming soon? If only my words were written in a book...but wait, they are! Job's words are in a book. God's words are in a book. My words are in a book. Your words are in a book of life. Each word you say has an impact as if it was chiseled in stone. You cannot take it back so choose it carefully. Lift up and don't put down. Pull up, don't crush carelessly. Look up and be sweet! That Day is coming where no tears will happen, no sadness, no cancer, no sorrow, no burdens...That Day is coming of no sickness, no pain, no parting...That Day when the clouds will roll back and instead of the sun, it will be The Son! I know that God lives! I would love to introduce you if you don't know Him! I am not waiting...Jesus is coming again....oh, how I long for That Day!

Because of this decision we don't evaluate people by what they have or how they look. We looked at the Messiah that way once and got it all wrong, as you know. We certainly don't look at him that way anymore. Now we look inside, and what we see is that anyone united with the Messiah gets a fresh start, is created new. The old life is gone; a new life emerges! Look at it! All this comes from the God who settled the relationship between us and him, and then called us to settle our relationships with each other. God put the world square with himself through the Messiah, giving the world a fresh start by offering forgiveness of sins. God has given us the task of telling everyone what he is doing. We're Christ's representatives. God uses us to persuade men and women to drop their differences and enter into God's work of making things right between them. We're speaking for Christ himself now: Become friends with God; he's already a friend with you.

2 Corinthians 5: 16-20

Fresh Start!

The new day is dawning as the new year rises and the hope of a fresh start swells inside. Excitement, hope, a new look, a fresh start all come at once with a choice. Once and for all, Jesus came and His supreme sacrifice, His decision to lay down His life for all mankind means that we are not to evaluate people by their looks or what they have but rather by looking at their heart and ties to the Messiah, for the fresh start comes through His sacrifice. God doesn't look at us and see one who had served years and another who only just chose to follow Christ, He looks upon us and sees the price of sin bought by the Blood of the Lamb. Truly there is reward for diligence and following Him in service and faithfulness at the Great White Throne Judgement but when we get to the end of our journey, the only way in is through the saving grace of Jesus Christ who has given to all the world the choice of the gift of life...but a decision must be made. The decision to let the old go and allow the new to emerge.

My youngest son is spending time with his future bride here at our home. Last night we played games and it was so sweet and revealing to watch them talk and choose together as they learn about each other. While we could simply look at our spouse or make a noise which they could interpret, they are still learning in the newness and freshness of first love. I always love the excitement on the faces of those in the newness of a relationship as they lean into the one they now love. It is with a special freshness and certainty that has never experienced disappointment. Love hurts and some disappointments of love hurt deeper and longer than others but God calls us to be free from it. Jesus made the decision to sacrifice His love in the Garden of Gethsemane...he waged a battle of self there and won. Once and for all, He settled the debt of sin but look at it...all this freshness comes with a price tag He paid which requires us to let go of the old to embrace the new. He calls us to settle or square up our relationships with others. He gives us the task of telling others what He is doing but we cannot be very effective at it if people see us as no different than the world. If the old man deals in politics and blasts others and we do the same on the opposite side, then how are we shining the light of Christ? Blasting others with our words and actions isn't Christlike and doesn't bring Him glory. If your purpose as a new creation is to show His love, then it should be obvious. There is no doubt to anyone who looks, that my boys are crazy about their girls and vice versa. If we are to persuade others to enter into God's work of making things right and we speak for Christ Himself then we better act like it in ALL we say and do. This means act with kindness, use His words not those nasty ones that come from the old creature, lift others up instead of criticizing-especially those we love but those in public also. Here's a question to look at: would God be ashamed of your actions, words, deeds? Ask this before you make choices: WWJD...what would Jesus Do? I know this became a fad and people say it without doing it but that is not the point. The purpose is a fresh mindset...a new start. If we are His hands extended and His mouthpiece, some of us need to wash up first because we have chosen to get dirty in our actions, words or deeds and it doesn't matter our role at Sunday services if our Monday actions stink. It doesn't matter who you are. You can be a preacher, a teacher, a politician who is well known, a rich man who has enormous influence or a poor one without a dime, we all must come into the freshness in the same manner and demonstrate His love in His calling. What are you doing to shine the light of first love to those around you?

"Up on your feet! Take a deep breath! Maybe there's life in you yet. But I wouldn't know it by looking at your busywork; nothing of God's work has been completed. Your condition is desperate. Think of the gift you once had in your hands, the Message you heard with your ears—grasp it again and turn back to God.

"If you pull the covers back over your head and sleep on, oblivious to God, I'll return when you least expect it, break into your life like a thief in the night.

"Look at me. I stand at the door. I knock. If you hear me call and open the door, I'll come right in and sit down to supper with you. Conquerors will sit alongside me at the head table, just as I, having conquered, took the place of honor at the side of my Father. That's my gift to the conquerors!

Revelation 3: 2-3, 20-21

Life in You Yet!

Yesterday got to me not in the way I thought. It was a day of pain and fear instead of a day of hope and renewal. My body and my heart inside me wanted to just crawl back into the covers and cry because my emotions were wrought and my heart was torn deeply. But God, who is always there and always will be, spoke His word to me through a sweet woman of God ministering at my church. Psalms 23. No matter where I go or what happens, the Lord is my shepherd. He stands directing and eager to save. He stands knocking at the door of hearts who choose to not listen but He patiently waits. I am a conqueror not because of anything I did but because of Him. Yesterday, He conquered the valley of the shadow of death in my life as He has many times before. His promises in Revelation 3 as He writes to the churches is that through it all, He is there and we will sit alongside Him at the head table if we remain in Him as conquerors. A conqueror is one who overcomes in the battle of life. We have lots of battles and some come from unexpected sources and some are devastating to us but He has called us into this battle and given us the tools. I will admit that the battle I waged came unexpectedly and from a place I never thought. I know I should have picked up my weapons, but I tried to war in the flesh with that which was a spiritual battle, and then I retreated, licking my wounds to a place of healing. Then He said, Get up on your feet and take a deep breath. Realize that He is God and we are His. Think of the Gift of Life and Love He has given us and that we have in our hands. If you put it down, you still have the opportunity to pick it back up. If you never truly held it, you still have the chance to do so. You have heard the Message with your ears and seen it with your eyes. It has been taught to you through the living example of those who have walked in Him around you whether you choose to accept it or not. You are in desperate condition without realizing it. Your life itself hangs in the balance and He holds the scales. Getting busy serving others and refusing time with Him or worse turning from Him in ignorance and doubt brings heartache and pain. Jesus is coming, and as a thief in the night while you sleep if you choose to ignore His knocking while it is yet day. You can ignore what He is saying for a time or you can yield and put your life to rights. God's work isn't busywork to keep your day from being boring. God's work on you may prevent you from being busy until you have dealt with that which He is calling you to deal with in your life. Being busy doing for others, serving in places and even meeting the needs without His love is worthless. How are you treating those around you in His love and service? Are you so self absorbed that you think only of you and have your head under the covers of warmth and security without realizing that you are shutting others out in the cold? Is your head so deep into your own needs and desires that you miss the moments of life He is speaking to you? Yesterday may have been a great day or a day like mine where God had to intervene to save your life from the pit of hell itself but either way, God is still knocking for you to open up fully to His presence. He cannot and will not dwell in a life full of selfish pride and knowing it all. He will empty you first so that He can come in to fill you once again. Open the door while there is time. There may still be some life in you, and He is knocking.

Trust God from the bottom of your heart;
don't try to figure out everything on your own.
Listen for God's voice in everything you do, everywhere you go;
he's the one who will keep you on track.
Don't assume that you know it all.
Run to God! Run from evil!
Your body will glow with health,
your very bones will vibrate with life!
Honor God with everything you own;
give him the first and the best.
Your barns will burst,
your wine vats will brim over.
But don't, dear friend, resent God's discipline;
don't sulk under his loving correction.
It's the child he loves that God corrects;
a father's delight is behind all this.

Proverbs 3: 5-12

Loving Correction!

I remember when my boys were little and they would get into trouble where I had to discipline them and I would hear them talking to themselves afterwards repeating the words I had told them. One particular time, I heard Gabriel saying, "she loves me, I know she does, I just cannot spit anymore" over and over getting the discipline set in his mind as discipline and not punishment. God doesn't punish us with no thought to what will come of tomorrow but God, the loving Father, does discipline us with a loving heart guiding us into correction for His glory and for our own sake. Resenting God's discipline is like resenting the rain. It is necessary to life and yet sometimes inconveniences come along with it. Flood watches, tornadoes, high winds, lightning strikes and loud thunderstorms come but all of these ultimately are just part of the natural processes God set in place thousands of years ago before our time. He knew our paths before we ever walked them and we are not alone. Listening to His voice instead of the voices of doubt, fear and confusion is the key. I played this game called trust when I was growing up and I have played it in Children's church where you have one person guiding a blindfolded kid throughout an obstacle course only by words but everyone else is trying to override those instructions by yelling out otherwise…only those who listen carefully and tune into the correct voice will make it through the course without bumbling around. This is an illustration of life and how we must tune into Him only. Recently I was listening to the radio when static and then other voices broke through and I realized I could hear someone's conversation over my radio… the tuning had picked up that channel and was now playing that instead of the channel I selected. Noisy voices, advice, criticism, directions, thoughts, ideas and suggestions will come at us from all directions but we must learn to lean in and tune into His voice alone for the others only lead to heartaches, frustration and downfall. We must learn who is speaking with His authority and who is just an opinionated person sharing their thoughts. We must learn to be gracious and merciful to others who advise while also being cautious with the advice we accept.

The track of God has good for us-brimming with health and life and when we honor God before all else, He blesses us with gifts overflowing our expectations. But the child He loves, He also disciplines and directs back to the path of life. I watched a sad story last night about a young couple who pulled over to the side of the road in a snowstorm just a couple of miles shy of their hotel. Then the blizzard came covering their car as they slept. Next the snowplow came piling it higher and higher each day not realizing they were there and they were too afraid to leave the car. The wife gave birth on about the 16th day and the husband gave all he had to keep the mother and child warm and fed until he passed away from cold and hunger on day 24. Finally after a month of being stuck, the mother climbed out through the snow realizing that though it appeared very deep, it wasn't that deep. As it started to thaw, she found she was right by the road and only a couple of miles later she was saved. The husband sacrificed his life giving all he had except conquering his fear of the unknown and lost his life because of that fear. Trusting God means that sometimes we will face a mountain of desperation that we have to fight through grief and frustration but He is there and He is clearing the path, making the way straight and easy. We just have to step out of our own cocoon of perception and into His way so that we can reach the place He has for us. We must fight through getting stuck in our own thoughts and ways by leaning into His word when the situation seems impossible. Trust God from the bottom of your heart. Trust in the Lord with all your heart. Lean into Him instead of your own understanding of things. In everything acknowledge His authority and power so that He will direct you and keep you. The surroundings look bleak and the place you are in seems ok and safe but perhaps it is time to step out into His place of authority to save ourselves. Only He knows where we are and what we are doing as well as where we are going. Only He knows the ins and outs of our future and will direct it in complete authenticity. Trust His loving correction and when we aren't sure, we must speak His words to ourselves to keep our minds right and set on Him just like my little boy affirmed my love for Him.

He loves us with an everlasting love and His course correction is for our own good!

This is God's Word on the subject: "As soon as Babylon's seventy years are up and not a day before, I'll show up and take care of you as I promised and bring you back home. I know what I'm doing. I have it all planned out—plans to take care of you, not abandon you, plans to give you the future you hope for.

Jeremiah 29: 10-11

As Soon As...!

My boys loved to go and do things socially and outside and I remember many a day telling them "as soon as" "this" happens then that can happen such as stating as soon as you clean your room we can go. That statement sets a standard of expectation to promise. It moves us beyond our perception to a reality. I see many people quote Jeremiah 29:11 without the "as soon as", because they either choose to ignore or think it is unimportant but as God is our Heavenly Father, I think all His words have depth and meaning especially these three words...as soon as. He states He knows what He is doing and He has it all planned out but it is as soon as... Babylon in this prophecy was a very real place of captivity and exile where God's people suffered for 70 years before their release. For many, they died in captivity at that time and others were born and lived their entire lives in captivity. It is likely that all of those who experienced the release and restoration were born in captivity. I find it interesting that the average life span now is 79 years. A child gets to the age of responsibility around age 9 then spends 70 years in captivity here on earth before experiencing the promise. We are so eager to see all of the promises in our lifetime but the reality is that we may not always see all of them. In 1948 Israel became a nation. God said that this generation would not pass before He returns but the truth is, that generation is approaching the average life span. We do not know the day and hour He will show up to take care of us as He promised and bring us back home but we do know it is close. Meanwhile, we also know His promises to care for us and to have a plan for us in the waiting place is also true. Restoration is powerful and God isn't eager for any to perish but wants all of us to have life. We are to hold onto the "as soon as", knowing that His promises are true and valid, tangible and strong. He hasn't abandoned us. We are His. We may have to walk through the "as soon as" in our own lives from cancer and sickness to finances and emotional stress but "as soon as" we have accomplished what He has set before us, the promise will be fulfilled. Pray today that God will reveal your "as soon as" to you so you might get diligent in doing what needs to be done to obtain His promise...it is there...as soon as....

"Give your entire attention to what God is doing right now, and don't get worked up about what may or may not happen tomorrow. God will help you deal with whatever hard things come up when the time comes.

Matthew 6: 34

Attention, Please!

Yesterday I worked with a student who was having trouble with focus and attention in the classroom and when we discussed what his biggest issue was, it was the distractions around him. People clamoring for his attention while he is trying to receive instructions kept pulling him off task and out of sorts then a big project would be introduced and he would feel overwhelmed having no idea where to start because his mind had been on something else while the teacher was discussing the subject. We all get this in the world today where everything is clamoring to steal our time and attention. We get so excited and worried about what will or will not happen day after day rather than just resting in Him. When our attention is cast in other directions, then we cannot see or hear what God is trying to tell us about the now because we are too distracted to take the time to focus on His word and His authority. Things happen that are time stealers and time wasters from iPads and iPhones to Facebook and Youtube to politics, television, debates and issues.

All of these time stealers take time from God. I see many people profess to love God but spend more time with their phone than with God's word. Recently as I sat at a friend's funeral, the pastor remarked on the Bible he had carried and how there were more scriptures marked than unmarked and I thought of what I knew of him....the Word was truly his life and legacy because he dwelled in it.

I challenged myself the next day to see where I spent my focus and attention...did I spend more time with Him or more time with my day to day issues...where was my focus? I found that by deliberately paying attention to where my focus was, I would direct my attention to where it needed to be. Just as I instructed the student yesterday. Where you focus is where your attention will be and you have that control. Yes, your brain and the world around you will try to steal your focus but greater is He that is in you. You have the ability to choose. You have the ability to lay down that thing that steals your time away from God and your family. Ask your family, what is the one thing I cannot live without? If they do not say God or His word, then your priorities have gotten skewed and you need to refocus your attention on where He desires you to be, centered-on Him. God is able to deal with anything that comes up. Your worry or attention on that thing or things over Him will not change one thing. Prioritize. God first. Family second. Others third. Yourself and selfish desires last. This doesn't mean to ignore your needs because God will not do that. He takes care of the birds of the air and will care for you. Put Him in control and prioritize His word and time with Him. Watch your life line up. I know I have some focus exercises to do now.

Jesus first, others next, yourself last to spell JOY.

Jesus said, "If you've had a bath in the morning, you only need your feet washed now and you're clean from head to toe. My concern, you understand, is holiness, not hygiene. So now you're clean. But not every one of you." (He knew who was betraying him. That's why he said, "Not every one of you.") After he had finished washing their feet, he took his robe, put it back on, and went back to his place at the table. Then he said, "Do you understand what I have done to you? You address me as 'Teacher' and 'Master,' and rightly so. That is what I am. So if I, the Master and Teacher, washed your feet, you must now wash each other's feet. I've laid down a pattern for you. What I've done, you do. I'm only pointing out the obvious. A servant is not ranked above his master; an employee doesn't give orders to the employer. If you understand what I'm telling you, act like it—and live a blessed life.

John 13: 10-17

Act Like It!

I've heard a saying that is supposedly associated with this scripture..."cleanliness is next to Godliness". But to be clear Jesus clearly states that in His act of washing the disciples' feet, it wasn't about hygiene but rather about holiness. Holiness gets misconstrued as being proper, spiritual or religious which is really almost an antonym in usage. Holiness is not a thing of pride but rather a place of servanthood. Learning to be a servant of all means being willing to do things in an unreciprocated and unrecognizable fashion. The cleanliness of spirit that Jesus was declaring was a willingness to lay it all down for Him. This is why He said Judas wasn't clean because he had come into the room planning to betray Jesus so he brought that evil spirit in with him to the place of worship and fellowship with Jesus. How often we are guilty of the same thing. We approach our time with God as a chore or requirement rather than a joy. We feel obligated or obliged to be there so we have an attitude of ingratitude and a flushed spirit. We feel set upon or irritated by expectations of others so we harbor that in our lives and carry it in our spirits. We approach the throne of God full of self and me needs. Jesus was teaching his disciples about laying it all down and becoming a grateful servant blessed to do the will of God no matter how lowly the task may seem or the appreciation factor. I grew up as a pastor's daughter so I saw all the tasks and expectations people lay upon their pastors. The bar set by my parents was high and hard for many of the pastors in my life to reach because some didn't seem to have the same level of conviction of servanthood. I loved and served them anyway because that is what I am called to do. We are not called to judge the fitness of the pastor nor his servanthood but rather to be the servant of Christ washing the feet of the disciples of Christ. We are called to serve, not judge.

This doesn't mean that they chew the food and we swallow it. It means that when we are provided a meal offering from God through the pastor, we take that meal and eat of it, digesting it slowly and carefully with plenty of the Living Water to help us understand and digest. When there are parts that are unrecognizable or indigestible, put them aside to pray and meditate on or even to discuss with the pastor whose authority you choose through God's leading to sit under for that time. A servant doesn't rank above a master nor an employee over their employer so we do not rank above the authority of Christ in the lives of others. Our role is to be a servant of God willing to do what He asks us to do and Jesus says that when we understand this and ACT like it, then we will live a blessed life. It is required for us to perform the tasks we are given through the spirit-tasks of holiness not hygienic ones. If God calls you to clean a toilet (and that call can be as simple as seeing the dirty toilet at church and thinking someone should clean this), then do it with joy as unto the Lord. God calls each of us for different purposes and tasks each of us at different times with callings....sometimes immediately like taking care of a situation that is dire and sometimes long term as a position of serving in the nursery, drama team, singing, playing music or other tasks of teaching, etc. Whatever He calls you to do-that your hand finds to do in serving Him-do it with all of you in joy as a servant of God for therein lies the opportunity to live a blessed life.

The act of Serving is the key that opens the door to walking in a blessed life.

Every God-born person conquers the world's ways. The conquering power that brings the world to its knees is our faith. The person who wins out over the world's ways is simply the one who believes Jesus is the Son of God.

1 John 5: 4-5

The Faith Power!

There is an infinite fascination with supernatural powers which is the focus of many a fairytale to the superheroes. Movies, television shows and lots of music, centers around the power of believing and changing our world but each one has a focus on the mystical or the supernatural in a magical way rather than the true power of the believer in God. The reason for this is our faith walk. When we walk in faith, we simply believe. We trust in the supernatural ability of God Himself working in us and through us and this is the conquering power that brings the world to its knees-this is faith. Faith isn't just a passive emotion but rather an action, a choice, an ability to walk in Supreme confidence knowing not what will happen but only that it will happen and it will be the right thing despite the circumstances and despite the cost. Faith can move mountains and change landscapes although we rarely understand this and we rarely speak of it in a physical sense because we do not invoke or use that level of faith very often. When my boys were little, they loved superhero capes. They would jump around the room, flying off the furniture and actively engaging their imagination in the possibilities of their mind. They were the superheroes of their own thoughts and imaginations which allowed them to perform feats completely beyond their own skills simply because they thought they could (and because their parents were there to protect and guide them). They learned that Jesus is the best superhero because He is always there, not waiting on the Bat signal nor the super hearing but there immediately at the whisper of His name in the time of need and when we are just going about our everyday tasks. He sticks closer than a brother and is our friend. He knows us more intimately than any other and He never fails us. Picture yourself as a superhero. Look into the mirror and see the potential that God has for you. Speak His word over your heart and mind deliberately. Let Him come in and fill you with His faith power then walk it out. It may not look like you expected it to look but it never does.

God's ways are not our ways but the cool thing is that His ways rock! Jesus is our superhero and He conquered death, hell and the grave. He gives us the super powers of faith, grace and mercy as well as peace and joy. We have all these superpowers at our discretion to use but we must employ them. It wouldn't help you to have a superpower that you never used and it always helps to use the right one and this is where His word and presence of the Holy Spirit guide us. If we know we are the conquerors and nothing can defeat us in the power of God, then why do we walk around like a beat up, stomped out piece of dirt? We are the superheroes! Our Savior has already conquered and made us winners! He gave us His supernatural strength to accomplish all things in His name. God gave us His supernatural peace to not let the troubles bother us, as He said "My peace, I give unto you...in this world you shall have trouble but be of good cheer for I have overcome the world." He gave us His superpower of blocking all attacks against us as He said "no weapon formed against you shall prosper". Claim His promises. These are your superpowers to activate the Faith Power which is the supreme power that makes us conquerors.

When Hathach told Mordecai what Esther had said, Mordecai sent her this message: "Don't think that just because you live in the king's house you're the one Jew who will get out of this alive. If you persist in staying silent at a time like this, help and deliverance will arrive for the Jews from someplace else; but you and your family will be wiped out. Who knows? Maybe you were made queen for just such a time as this."

Esther 4: 12-14

For Such a Time…!

This morning I read the books of Esther and Job thru twice. These stories are such important stories because they give us a picture of how God sees things far before and beyond what we do and they allow us to focus a little further afield than our current situation. We often get trapped into selfish thinking and wrapped into our ability or inability to do this or that but I read of Esther whose life had been changed drastically from what she expected. To some, her story is a fairytale of a common girl becoming queen. To some, her story is a sad one of an orphan kidnapped to be a pawn of a king. To the Jews, her story is one of salvation of her people and to some it is a story of a massacre of their people at the hands of the Jews. The point is that we all have personal perspectives or viewpoints as we look at these stories of Esther and Job. But God. God had a purpose and as stated by Mordecai, if Esther or Job had not done as God had ordained at that time, God would still have been God and still would have accomplished His purpose. The choice was theirs as it is ours to serve and walk in God's steps. Scripture tells us to rejoice for the steps of a righteous man are ordered by the Lord. We may feel left out or let down by God because we interceded, prayed, fasted, believed and yet things went differently than we had hoped.

We may feel bereft that God "failed us" in our wants and desires but the truth is that He doesn't fail. His plans are higher than our plans and we are not just pawns of a king but we are His beloved. We are the ones He wants so much more for than our limited minds can imagine. Who knows? Maybe we were put in our very situational settings for such a time as this. Maybe that waiting place is an important place for God to move in our lives. Maybe that financial struggle or that grief or that doubting of God's purpose were all designed as places of deliverance. I'm sure Moses never wanted to be in many of his situations nor did Joseph nor Job nor Mary/Joseph nor even the disciples. Each of us walks through difficult and different circumstances that no one else understands and sometimes we feel very let down and discouraged but it is time that we begin to shed a new light on it and say, "ok, God, I choose to see this as your purpose and your plan. I trust you to direct my path through this situation whether it be great blessings or severe disappointments because I trust you are God and you have me here for Such a Time as this. Direct me as you would have me to go and I will trust in you no matter what." The circumstances may seem bleak and impossible but God is bigger than what we see and more than what we feel. The walls may look impossible to climb and we may be called to swim when we don't know how…but dive in because God will direct you. He's called us For Such a Time… and we have the opportunity to be a part of something amazing even when it feels like we are in a bad situation or impossible place.

"Now it's time to change your ways! Turn to face God so he can wipe away your sins, pour out showers of blessing to refresh you, and send you the Messiah he prepared for you, namely, Jesus. For the time being he must remain out of sight in heaven until everything is restored to order again just the way God, through the preaching of his holy prophets of old, said it would be. Moses, for instance, said, 'Your God will raise up for you a prophet just like me from your family. Listen to every word he speaks to you. Every last living soul who refuses to listen to that prophet will be wiped out from the people.'

Acts 3: 19-23

Time to Change!

Each year people wake up to the fact that there are things in their lives they would like to change and they set resolutions or goals to make change but the truth is that the average person has already dropped the initiative to that change within ten days of making the goal. Statistics say that 68% of people do not make the changes they set out to make due to lack of discipline. Only about 9% of people who set a New Year Resolution follow through. We are not prone to changing our ways. We get into a set mind-frame and we choose to excuse our lack of follow through. In Acts, Paul says "Now, it's time to change your ways! Turn to God so He can wipe away your sins, pour out showers of blessing to refresh you and send you the Messiah he prepared for you, namely Jesus."

Jesus came to bring us new life by fulfilling the old covenant between God and man with a once in a lifetime sacrifice to end all others. He is/was the spotless Lamb that was slain for our sins so that we did not have to have the punishment and yet, we must decide to live in Him and abide in Him. We can no longer turn to our own ways or we will be turning away from God. Facing God brings about blessings but it also brings about discipline and change. One cannot aim to change their ways and lack discipline to do so while expecting blessings. Discipline is a key to change. While giving your life to God is instant and requires nothing but the turning to face Him, the keeping of your face towards Him and not being turned back around or distracted by other things requires the discipline of getting into His word and meditating on Him. One cannot expect change with no effort on their part. Animal instincts are strong and dogs have some nasty habits. I watch this sweet dog I have, turn into a different creature with some nasty habits whenever he is let loose to do as he pleases. Then when he returns to the house, he has to be cleaned and set straight. When he sets himself towards that which is not good for him and I call his name to direct his attention, he chooses to listen or disregard me. As he has aged, he has learned that discipline comes from me when he refuses to discipline himself. This is much the same with children and we are called the children of God because we are willful and stubborn but He loves us despite our ways. He calls to us to heed His voice and not go our own way as He knows our tendencies and minds. He knows we have nasty habits and poor discipline when we tend to go our way. He sees us for who we are and that is why He sent His son as a sacrifice for us. He knew there was no way for us to save ourselves for we are sin prone. He sent His son Jesus as an atonement for us so that we might be with Him. Notice that the wiping away of sin requires the turning to face God.

We cannot continue to ignore the call of His voice and roll in our own mucky, nasty ways expecting Him to wash us clean. His loving voice is chasing after us, calling to us but He has given us our own free will. He is calling us to repentance, to turning towards Him and facing Him so that He can cleanse us and bless us and refresh us. Time is drawing to a close when everything in Heaven will be prepared and the Messiah will come again to take His bride away but now is the time to listen to His voice calling us away from ourselves to turn to face Him fully so He can bless us and cleanse us.

God sacrificed Jesus on the altar of the world to clear that world of sin. Having faith in him sets us in the clear. God decided on this course of action in full view of the public—to set the world in the clear with himself through the sacrifice of Jesus, finally taking care of the sins he had so patiently endured. This is not only clear, but it's now—this is current history! God sets things right. He also makes it possible for us to live in his rightness. But by shifting our focus from what we do to what God does, don't we cancel out all our careful keeping of the rules and ways God commanded? Not at all. What happens, in fact, is that by putting that entire way of life in its proper place, we confirm it.

Romans 3:25-26, 31

Shifting the Focus!

God sets things right! We get so caught up in the me, my and mine that we forget who patiently endured our selfish ways and sent His own son as an atonement for our sin so that the law was met but the life fulfilled. God sacrificed Jesus publicly on the altar of sin-Jesus chose to put His will into the hands of the Father knowing it was going to be agony but willing to take this course of action to once and for all take care of the debt accumulated. Faith in this once and for all is what sets us right with God and He makes it possible for us to live in His rightness. The way of life before us is often unclear. A few days ago, while playing a game of questions, I asked my kids if they would prefer to go back to the past and meet ancestors or forward and meet progeny. They answered to go back because knowing the history of where you came from is important and this is exactly why we have the entire way of life recorded in the law books of history. History has value and teaches us from its mistakes so that we learn and do not make the same mistakes. If we erase history through the tearing down of the past, we make it virtually useless to our future knowledge of avoiding the same pitfalls. This photo is a replica of another photo I saw where the photographer has shifted her focus from the flame to the embers. This shift matters because it directs the focus into what is being broadcasted instead of what is being burned. What is the resulting outcome of our shifting the focus from what we are able to do or not, to what he is able to do? He, who exceedingly and abundantly gives before we think or ask. What happens if we shift our focus off of our lack onto His ability to provide for us? We begin to activate the faith as a grain of mustard seed. That small seed that has lain dormant producing nothing begins to wake up and say, it's time to trust God to be my source and my provider, my direction and my meaning. I don't have to tug, pull, worry and sweat about what may or may not happen but rather rely on Him who is the author and finisher of the faith to do what He has said He will do. I remember growing up there was this cartoon with these twins called the Wonder Twins and they had to put their hands together and say some silly rhyme but it was the action of them agreeing that caused the power to be available to them. We have that power we need in Jesus and when we align our lives in Him, His provision is enough. He makes ways where there seems to be no way, parts seas so we can walk on dry ground and produces miracles from the air. Shift your focus! We gotta Quit trying to do it on our own! We need to allow Him to be God. Getting it in line with him allows that Wonder Faith to activate!

No man shall be able to stand before you all the days of your life; as I was with Moses, so I will be with you. I will not leave you nor forsake you. Be strong and of good courage, for to this people you shall divide as an inheritance the land which I swore to their fathers to give them. Only be strong and very courageous, that you may observe to do according to all the law which Moses My servant commanded you; do not turn from it to the right hand or to the left, that you may prosper wherever you go. This Book of the Law shall not depart from your mouth, but you shall meditate in it day and night, that you may observe to do according to all that is written in it. For then you will make your way prosperous, and then you will have good success. Have I not commanded you? Be strong and of good courage; do not be afraid, nor be dismayed, for the Lord your God is with you wherever you go."

Joshua 1: 5-9

God's Commission!

The waiting place is a hard place to be and often involves a lot of self-doubt. Uncertainty drives us as humans to make choices that often we regret because we rush into things by not seeing the value of the waiting place. Joshua stood with Moses as a young man against many complaints and now Moses has charged him with leading the people to the promised land and blessed him. Joshua felt uncertain and unsure until God came and commissioned him. He knew Moses had gone into the mountains but God buried Moses so no one knows where he is. Joshua is just a young man who got his degree of training under Moses but he was untried as far as being a leader so he was uncertain but God...we love these scriptures of Joshua's commission Be strong and of good courage, do not be dismayed for God is with you wherever you go but I wonder if we shouldn't look a little deeper. Before that conclusion that we love to quote is the commission. God told Joshua not to turn from His word to the right nor left (this includes politics) so we May prosper wherever we go. He said His book should not depart from our mouths and we should meditate in it day and night so that we may observe to do what is written there to make us prosperous with good success. Wow! What a commission! When you are commissioned to do something, you are given specific instructions on how to carry out a task, goal or project. These are God's specific instructions to lead us to prosperity and success. I've read many self-help books on business success and how to get the right marketing and mindset for business but the truth is finding the right commission is the key. God gives us each a personal commission. He charged us all with going into the world-our market-place-and sharing Him with all we meet. He gave us the tools and He gave us the means, provides the opportunities and then sees what we do with His son, Jesus. Joshua had a spectacular commission that we like to borrow as it lifts us up but we have the great commission from Jesus Himself that tells us to Go into all the World and teach the gospel. If you are in a waiting place in life, waiting for the next road, path, uptick in your journey...perhaps today is a good day to employ the word of God and set forth on the Great Commission. Joshua's job was to lead a group of people into the Promised Land and this is your job too. God has called each of us to lead those in our realms of influence into The Promised Land of Heaven through introducing them to His son, Jesus. This is the way of prosperity and success. This is the path He has called us to do. He will be with you. He will never leave you nor forsake you. Be strong and courageous in Him. Do not be discouraged but rather remember in your waiting place that God has given you His greatest commission yet and if you are achieving that, He is preparing the path ahead for prosperity and success. The key is to meditate on Him and His words. Ask Him to provide you with a personal commission from Him. He will.

"How can I account for this generation? The people have been like spoiled children whining to their parents, 'We wanted to skip rope, and you were always too tired; we wanted to talk, but you were always too busy.' John came fasting and they called him crazy. I came feasting and they called me a boozer, a friend of the misfits. Opinion polls don't count for much, do they? The proof of the pudding is in the eating."

Matthew 11: 16-19

Proofed!

Preparing a book, article or ad requires proofing because mistakes are made by many and all at some point. Opinions are prevalent and everyone has one which is subject to change constantly. Jesus was frustrated with the people who were constantly whining and complaining of what they had or didn't have much like God had gotten frustrated with the Children of Israel as they whined. I have two children and I work with children every day. Lots of things affect them in their moods and actions. Some of them are worse than others in their actions as they struggle to do things that are hard and laborious which they do not know how to do, it is common for them to complain or whine. Their behavior improves as their ability improves. When you are able to do things without difficulty, it is easier to do and even more enjoyable. I do not like doing dishes or laundry but I am capable of doing it so there isn't a point in whining or complaining about it. When I was unable to do it because of my back, I complained about the pain it caused me as I tried to do it. Jesus compares this generation to spoiled children whining to their parents because He is trying to explain that opinion polls or what we think about our situations do not change the situation but rather doing the work does. When whining and complaining, we accomplish little but if we dig in and do the task, the enjoyment comes from the outcome. The proof of good cooking comes from eating the wonderful pudding made by following the recipe. Whining about how hard it is to cook it or to get the ingredients doesn't accomplish anything. Trusting that when it is all done-this work that Christ is doing in us-it will be delicious and perfect! Jesus knows, and knew the recipe-the way of the Cross wouldn't be easy. Knowing all as He did, it is amazing that He had the patience to listen to the whining and complaining but He knew that it would be worth it all when He had accomplished the recipe. The recipe for forgiveness was very hard and difficult but He accomplished it without whining and completely because He knew that citing the word over His complaints was the way through. The way through is to go through the hard, into the overcoming. It will be worth it all when we see Jesus.

Planning a wedding requires a lot of coordination and things to fall into place. There are many details to be seen about, but when it all comes together, it is beautiful and memorable. The marriage doesn't require all the pomp and circumstance but it is enjoyable & memories are made because of those things. Life is preparation for the wedding feast of the Lamb to the Bride (which is us). We are called to prepare ourselves and take care of the details of keeping our lives on track. He has given us the recipe of His word and where we are to get the ingredients to prepare ourselves by spending time with Him. It doesn't matter what the whiny children of the world say, He is coming again soon and it is time to stick close to the details of His recipe of life. The proof will be in His return and then it will be too late. Are you ready? Are you preparing, gathering the lost at all cost, reading and sharing His word? It is time to focus on the recipe and not the frustrations or opinions of those around us who naysay. The proof is in the outcome and He is on His way!

Whoever goes hunting for what is right and kind finds life itself— glorious life!

Proverbs 21: 21

Gone Hunting!

Today I went hunting but not for game or fish. Today I went hunting for what is right and kind. Today I have hunted all day. I have heard a lot of complaints and a lot of whining. I have seen a lot of pain and sorrow. I have seen so much and heard so much but I found the right and kind which is life itself too. We often get bogged down in our "to dos", and our day to day and we fail to do the hunting to find a glorious life. I will admit that today was a very hard day for me on a lot of levels from personal to business to finance to health...I had my share of woes but I also had my share of finding right and kind. Who was I today? I was the hunter and my prey was life outside the norm and it started in prayer this morning. I found kindness, rightness and love in my sweet husband as he kissed me good morning and said he was headed out for a day of hunting. Then I opened the scripture and decided I would hunt too. When a hunter goes hunting, he plans and puts out bait or plants to draw the deer in. So I decided to bait my day with prayers and with what is right and kind to see if I too could find life. I cannot say that my day went perfectly nor can I say it went according to my plan but I can say I found life. I found it in the kindness of strangers assisting an elderly woman on her walker who had locked her keys in her car at the post office. I found it in the sweet smile of the server at the restaurant I chose to visit and in the kind greeting of the bank teller. I found it in the joyful laugh of the delivery driver at my dog's antics, and in my neighbors as we walked and talked. I found it in my parents' sighs of relief after the PetScan although they still had a journey ahead and hadn't eaten all day. I found joy, kindness, and rightness wherever I looked because I was hunting it. Whatever you go hunting for, you will find it if you look hard and long enough. If you look for evil, it is there but so is the kindness. It all depends on what you are searching for in your day.

So today as I close out my day, I continue to hunt for what is right and kind because I want to find life-glorious life!

This is what God says, the God who builds a road right through the ocean, who carves a path through pounding waves, The God who summons horses and chariots and armies—they lie down and then can't get up; they're snuffed out like so many candles: "Forget about what's happened; don't keep going over old history. Be alert, be present. I'm about to do something brand-new. It's bursting out! Don't you see it? There it is! I'm making a road through the desert, rivers in the badlands. Wild animals will say 'Thank you!' —the coyotes and the buzzards— Because I provided water in the desert, rivers through the sunbaked earth, Drinking water for the people I chose, the people I made especially for myself, a people custom-made to praise me.
Isaiah 43:16-21

Dessert Road!

When I first typed the title, I hit too many letters but as I went back to correct it, God stopped me and said it is rightfully true. I don't know about you but I love a good dessert after a meal or even instead of a meal! It's like a reward party or a celebration in my mouth! Do you see it already? The pink road across the blue sky...the leading edge of the canvas of beauty, the road leading to Heaven marked in a brushstroke of beauty: God's road through your desert place. This is the same God who made a road in an impossible place of the ocean. The Israelites had departed Egypt and walked a long path in excitement for new beginnings until they heard the news traveling around their community that the Pharaoh and his troops had a change of heart...then fear set in stealing their joy, snuffing out their hope and turning them from triumphant conquerors into a whiny people. But God...God carved a path right through the pounding waves by stacking that water back like an invisible dam and drying the path right before their eyes. He led His people safely through then snuffed out their enemy in one fell swoop of crashing waves. They were snuffed out like candles and disappeared from the Earth at least until historians discover their remains one day.

But God continued. Even though His people soon forgot and turned away again, God continued. He even told them not to look back at old history but to look forward to the new things He was doing. As they moved from the place of conquering, to fear, to celebrating, to doubting, to triumph, to neglecting, these people much like us are a roller coaster of emotions. They failed to see the God who is, was and will be and allowed their circumstances to dictate their emotions rather than to trust, no matter what they see, that God can make a way. He tells us to be alert and present...not stuck in the past, not worrying about the future for He is about to do something brand new! The road in the desert is the dessert. Jesus. He is our living water in the desert of life. He custom made us for the express purpose of praising Him and it is in that praise that we see the road in the desert place and realize it is the dessert. A desert is dry and dusty, but even there, life teems with the right circumstances. Our place of life right now may feel like scorched earth, dry and sunbaked but the rain of God that comes from praise is on the horizon. This dessert place will soon be teeming with life in a brand new, bursting out kinda way. We have been chosen, designed, designated and purposed to worship. The long road of desert place, is poised to become a dessert place full of sweet rewards. Don't you see it? There it is! The road through our place of sorrow, pain, sickness, defeat, and struggle. It's all in the power of praise which unlocks the windows of Heaven to the mighty rain of God. The living water flows deeply and the way is there...be alert, be present for God is about to do mighty things in us when we begin to praise in our desert place! Yum! Taste and see that God is good and His mercies endure through All generations!

Hurry with your answer, God!
I'm nearly at the end of my rope.
Don't turn away; don't ignore me!
That would be certain death.
If you wake me each morning with the
sound of your loving voice,
I'll go to sleep each night trusting in you.
Point out the road I must travel;
I'm all ears, all eyes before you.
Save me from my enemies,
God—you're my only hope!
Teach me how to live to please you,
because you're my God.
Lead me by your blessed Spirit
into cleared and level pastureland.

Psalms 143: 7-10

Hurry with the Answer!

We live in a world of rush and hurry so it was with a laugh and smile that I read my exact thoughts this morning in David's Psalms. He too, felt that urgency of life pushing him while he barely hung on wondering what to do next. He too had tied a knot at the end of his rope and was hanging on for dear life. He is imploring God to not turn away or ignore him because he has felt that before.

Elephant in the room: why do people quote the scripture that God never leaves nor forsakes you when you are going through hard times and need help-when you already feel left out by God and deserted? Feelings and emotions are real but not always accurate. I can say this with all of my heart because I have been on steroids lately and boy oh boy do those things mess with your emotions, hormones and the swings...

Most people are truly trying to help and encourage when they quote scripture because they don't know what else to say. They feel awkward saying yea, it looks like your situation stinks and God may or may not pull you out of this mess you got yourself into but He will walk through it with you even though it is a tough trial. Those are hard words. I mean how do we wrap our brains around cancer and all the horrid things that come with it? Even more, how do we wrap our brain around cancer happening to someone who has served God faithfully and fully? What about when they survive it once then it reoccurs or if they die from it? I have seen this lately in both cases. It is mind boggling that a God who healed the lepers at a word, did not heal my precious friend who so believed and his family held on believing for him until he chose to step into Heaven. Hey God, where are you? What do I tell these kids who just lost their grandfather but they were holding on in faith? David fought this same dilemma. David said just wake me each morning with the song of your voice and I'll go to sleep each night trusting you. I will listen, look and follow your paths and your road just please save me... desperate here waiting...You're the only hope God. Ever felt that? Just needing a place to rest from the chase? Desiring a good soft time without struggle? David's prayer was just this...lead me God into cleared and leveled pastures. Don't make me continue to struggle up and down these mountains for a little bit of grass and a little moisture here and there but find me a place I can lie down and rest from all these trials. I "so" feel David in these scriptures as I have been there and am there. Chronic illnesses and back issues, financial stress and worry, constant pressure from work and home...all these everyone is experiencing. I know we look around and it seems others have it better but it's a facade. We are all struggling but the place of rest isn't found in this world. The place of rest is in the trusting. Yesterday I asked my staff to help me get the word out that trustworthiness is what the world (ie Google algorithm) is looking for on the web searches. The web crawler is looking to give you sites when you search that people have rated highly for trustworthiness. No falseness or fake data but a place you can trust and anchor to in a world full of fraud and deceit. The world at large searches for someone to be real with them. Just tell us the truth and show us Your (God's) power and might! Hurry God! We are desperate for You! We are clinging to this rope of promises from your word. We are believers who are believing! We are receivers who are ready to receive! We are eager for You! The world around us is so unreliable and the pressure is unrelenting both now and then whether you are a king or a man on the run for his life as David was both. These struggles aren't new. We aren't the first nor the last to have them. This overwhelming feeling of loss and frustration at life and God isn't new. It's been around and it's ok. Trusting God and being disappointed happens. It shakes you to the core. Job instructed us to "give thanks in everything" and Paul added "because it was the will of God through Christ Jesus in You". Both these men lived many "Hurry up God" moments and times where it seemed God had failed or let them down, but we can look back and see that God had purpose. We do not always understand but we can let it go and trust His hand. Teach us God, to please You even when our lives seem to be hanging on by a thread, that You have prepared a quiet place of rest in You, where the table is spread. The picnic is laid out on the quiet rolling hill by the waterfall to soothe our troubled minds and hearts. All we have to do is walk through it, in Praise, into that place of rest. We trust You no matter what it looks like...but Please Hurry God!

So don't turn a deaf ear to these gracious words. If those who ignored earthly warnings didn't get away with it, what will happen to us if we turn our backs on heavenly warnings? His voice that time shook the earth to its foundations; this time—he's told us this quite plainly—he'll also rock the heavens: "One last shaking, from top to bottom, stem to stern." The phrase "one last shaking" means a thorough housecleaning, getting rid of all the historical and religious junk so that the unshakable essentials stand clear and uncluttered.

Do you see what we've got? An unshakable kingdom! And do you see how thankful we must be? Not only thankful, but brimming with worship, deeply reverent before God. For God is not an indifferent bystander. He's actively cleaning house, torching all that needs to burn, and he won't quit until it's all cleansed. God himself is Fire!

Hebrews 12: 25-29

Active Fire!

Recently I was at a location for a meeting and the fire alarm began to peel loudly so I immediately jumped up, beginning to grab my things and everyone else continued on. As I started out of the room, the woman close to the door said, "sweetheart, it does that all the time, you can just ignore it" and I thought, wow, if a real fire happens, they will burn because they have grown immune to the alarm. Their ears have become deaf to the warnings because the alarm sounded falsely so often. I think of Christians who have heard for so many years that Jesus is coming soon and they too have grown complacent to the tones of warning. They hear them but their spirit is no longer stirred. They read them but mark it down as heard over and over. His voice once shook the foundations of Earth causing a massive earthquake and terrifying the people of Israel for they had turned their back on Him while waiting for Moses to come down from the mountain with the books of the law. He told us in His word that the next shaking will be top to bottom even rocking Heaven and will be the final shaking. This last shaking is a time of great housecleaning as everything false is destroyed once so that His kingdom stands unshakable in its foundations. This shaking occurs with the coming of Jesus as the Messiah. Fire is fascinating for it is not a discerner. It burns all in its path. What has been burned is cut off and renewal only comes from newness or really deep roots. God Himself is a cleansing fire that burns away the clutter and unusable so that the purity of the goodness is revealed. When foresters work to prevent careless fires, they do a controlled burn of cleansing fire to take out all the scrub brush that is dry tinder waiting for a spark. They purposelessly light a torch that they can walk through an area and burn loose debris and scrub that is dross waiting for an ember so that they can better protect that which should be saved. God is more than a simple forester or firefighter. He sees the built up gunk leading to the flames of hell in our lives and He deliberately torches things in our lives that limit us or will cause us to catch an ember of hell and ignite. He wants us to be fireproofed from the flames of hell because He knows the tricks and traps of the enemy.

He knows what the unshakable essentials are in us and He knows the junk.

Confessions: I am a little bit of a closet packrat. I don't like a lot of visible clutter but I tend to fill the junk drawer and cabinets easily to become junk cabinets. I have lots of stuff and likely if you need something, I have it but one day my husband looked for coffee in the storage where I keep some extra stuff. There were lots of coffee containers in there but each one he found was full of laundry lint. (Ok, I am not weird and I am not a hoarder but I had read that laundry lint was a great fire starter and we liked to have fire-pit wiener roastings with the kids and s'mores so I thought, easy fire starter would be cool.) Needless to say, those dozen or so coffee containers full of lint made a very fragrant bonfire shortly thereafter. I had been collecting something in my mind that was useful and purposeful; taking up space in my home and putting time and effort into a fire starter which truly would have been a huge fire hazard but with my open mind & heart focused on what I was doing, I never saw the danger or hazard, only the usefulness! I share that because this is what we do in our everyday lives. We are clutter collectors of things we think we may need or have usefulness to us in future without measuring it against the hazards or dangers it can be causing in our lives. We waste a lot of time on things that lead us nowhere and only stack up as potential threats to our future without realizing what we are doing. We throw out word salads toward others on social media and praying hands. We lamely look at the world around us as our daily collective instead of realizing that a fire is coming! It is time to clean away the clutter of our lives and purify our hearts before God. It is time to remove the fragrant fluff we have been collecting to ease us along as this will be the flame collector that will consume us. We see the results in our children from cellphones and the havoc they have wreaked in our homes. It is time for revival, fresh anointing and true renewal with all the dross and ember catchers to be burned away in our lives. If it isn't about God and His purpose, it is a potential fire starter that can catch the embers of hellfire and burn our lives down around our ears. Yes, that time spent on video games can be an ember catcher to burn your marriage up in smoke! Yes, that fascination with your ipad and the political morass can be an ember catcher burning the lives of those around you blinding you to their needs and making you into someone you never intended to be. Yes, your set ways of doing things or your complete disregard for another can be the lint that ignites the relationship to burn down between family members. How do we know what will catch the flame of God versus the flames of hell? Test it against His word. Pray over it and cover it in Living Water. God can ignite His fire through Living Water-just read Elijah's story! Time to remove the fire starters from your lifestyle if they can catch an ember of hell. Galatians 4:5-6. The fireproof test. Think on these things.

Now this is the confidence that we have in Him, that if we ask anything according to His will, He hears us. And if we know that He hears us, whatever we ask, we know that we have the petitions that we have asked of Him.

1 John 5: 14-15

The Confidence!

We have a puppy, well, really a dog as he is almost eight years old but he's a small dog, anyway....he knows he can get my attention with a small whine or bark. He is confident in my attention but less confident about anyone else. He has me trained! He has a confidence in who I am to him and believe me he has trained a neighbor or two also for treats! My dog doesn't always get exactly what he wants when he asks or whines but if it's within my power and I do not feel it will be bad for him or that the timing is right, I acquiesce. My children have much more access to me and can ask of me anything with the same confidence but as we grow into adulthood, we seem to acquire a negative impart into asking of our parents. We want to stand on our own, independent and strong. The familiarity becomes less as we move into our own ways and we are less confident of the willingness of our parents because we know them less. I would say I know my parents pretty well as I talk to them daily but the truth is that the "knowing" comes from spending time with someone. The "knowing" is what brings confidence to a relationship. I am always fascinated when I tell my children about other kids they spent years with when they were little and they look at me like I have three heads. They have no idea who I am talking about because they were young and the "knowing" has passed. The intimacy of those hours, days, and months are forever etched into my mind as the parent but they have lost the knowing and have no confidence in my memory because they have no relationship. I have drawn a lot of pictures for us to grasp the truth of this verse. The confidence we have in God comes from the Knowing of Him. Knowing in scripture indicates intimacy and relationship. When it says a woman knew a man, it means they were intimately involved. When we know God, we are intimately involved with Him and this brings a confidence to the relationship. Uncertainty in a relationship comes from newness, lack of trust or simply not knowing the person intimately because we haven't spent enough time together. God isn't willing that any should die and He sent His son to save all mankind but many do not know Him enough to ask. I cannot even imagine walking up to a stranger requesting them to give their life for me and yet, He already did. He knew us before we knew ourselves. He was willing to sacrifice His son, His very lifeblood for an atonement once and for all before we were born knowingly. This is our confidence. His promises still stand. He knew us intimately before we knew Him and yet was still willing to give His life. Peace doesn't come from a lack of storms in our lives but rather from the confidence in Him, the knowing that no matter how bad the storm, He is holding us. If we ask anything in His name, according to His will, He hears us and if we have confidence that He hears us then we know that whatever we ask, He will do. This is the intimate confidence of knowing Him. I know no one else that I can rely on to that level. No matter how strong or confident your parents are or your spouse or your BFF, they will fail you and let you down or be unable to be there for you completely in all situations. God, His son-Jesus, the Holy Spirit is closer than your breath and when you feel completely alone and bereft, He's there. Breathe Him in. Know Him. Dive deep into His word. Begin to praise in the middle of your story and there in that moment, He will be there in that knowing bringing the confidence of peace.

But you, Timothy, man of God: Run for your life from all this. Pursue a righteous life–a life of wonder, faith, love, steadiness, courtesy. Run hard and fast in the faith. Seize the eternal life, the life you were called to, the life you so fervently embraced in the presence of so many witnesses.

1 Timothy 6: 11-12

Seize Life!

Exciting news propels us to run towards it! When we look forward to something we are eager to embrace it, take hold of it and pursue it. We had a wonderful little dog who loved chasing a ball. I mean he was quite talented with bouncing the ball on his head and running it around the yard. It was quite the show! All you had to say was "let's play ball" and kick it. He would pursue that ball with his entire being all over the yard until he was exhausted but if you kicked it again, he would get up and go again. Paul is admonishing Timothy in this passage in the same way. Timothy has been running after God but has gotten discouraged and tired with a lot of naysayers. Paul admonished him to run away from all the garbage and pursue righteousness. Paul describes a righteous life as one of wonder, faith, love, steadiness and courtesy. I cannot help but picture a relay runner being handed a baton and told to run hard and fast to cinch the win! Seizing life is more than just approaching each day passively but rather diligently and passionately pursuing it. A prize doesn't come from doing nothing and Paul tells us that we are working towards the prize of the high calling. This prize is awarded as we pursue the faith, the race of life lived in the eternal perspective and embrace with all our being. One of my favorite shows of all times is Chariots of Fire. It is the story of a young man who pursues God through running and ends up winning the 1924 Olympic gold medal because he stayed true to what God directed him to do despite naysayers. His life after the movie is one of sacrifice and service as a missionary and he is martyred in a prison camp for his faith. His story isn't new but it is unique in that he literally pursued God through actual running. Pursuit is giving all you have towards the end goal which is the highest calling from Jesus with a heavenly reward. We have been called to a life of greatness in Him. A life of wonder and transformation filled with faith, renewed daily in His love, and steeped in the steadiness of His presence leads to a life of courtesy (polite speech and actions) for eternity.

Living a life of wonder is living with an air of expectation instead of an air of defeat. Faith opens doors that seemed to not exist until the magic of God's love reveals them. If you are looking in the wrong direction, you will not see. God doesn't play hide and seek with His presence nor His promises. He doesn't choose His favorite to bless and ignore another. It is all about our pursuit. His goodness and mercy are following us all our lives but we must choose to run fast and faithfully in Him with love filled wonder and faithful steadiness allowing His courtesy to become ours. His word & His actions become ours as we choose to be His hands and feet extended towards others.

Seize the prize-the wonder-the eternal life in Christ Jesus!

I love you, God—
you make me strong.
God is bedrock under my feet,
the castle in which I live,
my rescuing knight.
My God—the high crag
where I run for dear life,
hiding behind the boulders,
safe in the granite hideout.

Psalms 18: 1-2

Our Knight!

Thoughts swirl and twirl in our minds which many times overwhelm us like clouds covering the sun. We get caught up in our own blizzard of thoughts and the snowstorm of possibilities and emotions swirl around us blinding us to the truths in God's word. We are bombarded with man's philosophy and everything vying for our attention until we feel completely out of control. David felt the same thing. He had tried it His way and was feeling the thunder of life surrounding him warning the storm was on the horizon as he called out "I love you God"! He continues to lift God up in his voice and song of praise because he understands the power of that praise. If you are caught in a blizzard and cannot be seen, the best way to be found is to call out or sing so someone can hear and rescue you!! Of course as a female, I get the rescuing knight analogy but David is a very outdoorsy guy. He's calling for a fighting knight to do battle and protect. He understands that there are forces he cannot battle on his own and that God is his sheltered place and hidden place of rest. David first says he loves God and God makes him strong. Then he compares God to the bedrock or mountain under his feet. A bedrock is a foundational stone that is not affected by storms or weather or situations because it is the core of the foundation. It is the central building stone that is unmoved and immovable. God makes us strong by being our strength but not only that, God is the castle where we dwell. So here we have this description of God as a high, strongly built castle which is impenetrable and immensely immune to any attack founded on an immovable bedrock in which we live. But when we venture out from the safe castle of God into places of danger, God becomes our rescuing knight who saves us and delivers us as long as we run to His protection. He is the high point-the tip of the mountain crag or hiding place where boulders of His mercy and grace protect us from the arrow of the enemy for we are surrounded on all sides by His love as a shield of granite in a hideout of His peaceful presence. Yesterday as I listened to people around me panicking and crying on the airplane as it shook, rattled and rolled through a vicious storm, I realized that I had no worry. My whole spirit was at peace in complete confidence that He is in control no matter what may come my way. He isn't surprised, not taken aback. He is the stone fortress of our lives. We just must choose to allow Him to rescue us and take us under His wings of love. I love you God! You make me strong! I am thankful you are my knight in shining armor in all situations and I am grateful for your shield of mercy and grace, your weapon of salvation and your castle of love! Help me to focus my mind on you as I run from all that is thrown at me. I call out to you to rescue me from my blizzard of emotions and be my bedrock.

So let God work his will in you. Yell a loud no to the Devil and watch him make himself scarce. Say a quiet yes to God and he'll be there in no time. Quit dabbling in sin. Purify your inner life. Quit playing the field. Hit bottom, and cry your eyes out. The fun and games are over. Get serious, really serious. Get down on your knees before the Master; it's the only way you'll get on your feet.

James 4: 7-10

Yell No! Whisper Yes!

Ever had one of those days where everything seems to be going wrong or at least being very difficult? This is when we need to make our stand! Whisper "Jesus" then scream "Not today Satan" at the top of your lungs-better go outside if you are at work! Let God speak over you in His sweet peace. When it feels like everything is falling apart and the bottom is coming up fast...stretch out the parachute of God's love through praise and watch the winds of His glory fill the places of emptiness in you. Go ahead and have a good cry and purify your inner life so that the things that have distracted you from Him and caused you to "play the field" instead of giving it all to Him can crash and burn. Get serious with Him-like down on your knees, desperately seeking Him and watch Him rise up in you! He is the lifter of your head and only when you begin to struggle do you truly see that He is your source!

Let's get our steps in here to be healthier and happier! Here we go!
Let God work His will in You! Let's start this workout with some praise!
Stop trying to have it your way! Just do it! It works! Ok begin to whisper...Jesus, Jesus...
Whisper Jesus with all of your inner being! Ok...now fill those lungs...head outside where you can scream loud! Scream NO to the Devil at the top of your lungs! Do it again! Maybe two or three times more!

Now whisper Jesus again! Jesus! Jesus!

Get down on your knees!

Cry out to God to be your source!

Repent and refresh!

Now, Get up!

He's got you!

Chin up! Faith set!

Whisper Thank you Jesus!

Now get back to the mission He called you to do knowing He has it all under control!

Yes, that was me you heard hollering Not today Satan!

Mortals make elaborate plans,
but God has the last word.
Humans are satisfied with whatever looks
good; God probes for what is good.

We plan the way we want to live,
but only God makes us able to live it.

The road of right living bypasses evil;
watch your step and save your life.

It pays to take life seriously;
things work out when you trust in God.

Proverbs 16: 1-2, 9, 17, 20

Pay Day!

Unlike the candy bar by the same name, pay day is the day of receiving what is due for the work performed on a job or in life. Putting effort and hard hours in, results in getting only a portion of what you worked for because taxes and other things are deducted prior like insurance, retirement, etc. Many times that first day of pay is disappointing because we spent that money in our head and then the actual pay is a lot less due to these deductions. Solomon shared some of his pay in this chapter of Proverbs. When God asked Solomon for what he wanted and God would give him anything he desired, he asked for wisdom which God blessed him with as well as the riches because God loved his heart. Solomon wasn't a perfect person despite his wisdom because he too lived being satisfied with what looked good rather than instantly knowing what is good. God probes our hearts and minds to find what is good and he instructs us in Galatians to dwell or think on things that are good. Search and seek these because the negative thoughts tear us down and just like Esau we are too easily satisfied for immediate gratification rather than waiting and probing for the ultimate good. We are by nature planners of our future with elaborate thoughts and dreams but ultimately it is God who has probed those and mined for the gold which He leads us towards. Recently lots of people in my life have received bad news or not received the news they wanted about things from health to wealth to jobs and future hopes. Disappointing news or lack of expectations met, easily discourages us because we dream often without resting in His knowing. The road of right living is narrow and because we cannot often see the twists and turns, we plan the way we want to go not expecting the detours often brought into our life by God because He sees the cliffs or pitfalls of our plans. He probes for what is good while we are just satisfied with how it looks not realizing that the sinkhole will twist us up. The pay day to right living is when you take life seriously enough to trust that God will work all things out for good. He doesn't withhold. Watching our steps and consulting Him constantly on our journey results in a safe trip and a good life directed by the Master along an uphill course. Even though the path may be tough and look tough, He knows our best way. He will have the last word anyway so why not just trust Him? I laughed recently as I was on a trip to an unknown area and I relied on a GPS system although I know better from past experience. Sure enough it led me in circles to get to where I was going so I thought as I left, I'd go the more direct route I could see. What I couldn't tell was that the road was caved in on that direct path. It looked straightforward but it wasn't the right way. The path of circling wasn't being led astray but rather the path of safety. Sometimes we are so eager to get what we want, that we jump in without considering what God wants. This is when we deduct on our pay day because we chose to ignore or not consult the boss. We created a mess of our own making then we holler out to God to please fix our mess. He hears us and rescues us. His grace is so sufficient that He doesn't hold that against us or keep us from receiving all He promised. We keep ourselves from receiving the joy He would have us to walk in because we forget to consult Him before we proceed. What is the key to working and walking in a great life with no deductions from our pay day? Trust in Him with all our hearts and not leaning in our own way and Acknowledging Him in all our ways so that He directs our path. (Proverbs 3:5-6). Pay Day is coming for all of us on this journey of life. Jesus already paid the price of entry to the reward. We have only to live in God's truth and allow Him to guide us so we are not misdirected by our own ways. If a door doesn't open, it's not your door. Don't try to force it or make it happen. Pray about it and watch God work. He has a plan for you. Trust it and trust Him!

Then Jesus went to work on his disciples. "Anyone who intends to come with me has to let me lead. You're not in the driver's seat; I am. Don't run from suffering; embrace it.

Follow me and I'll show you how. Self-help is no help at all. Self-sacrifice is the way, my way, to finding yourself, your true self. What kind of deal is it to get everything you want but lose yourself? What could you ever trade your soul for?

Matthew 16: 24-26

Driver's Seat!

Last night was an adventure because of a key. The key was misplaced which caused several people to have to drive, meet up and pass the key to open a door. The self-sacrifice in order to help the other person came from a willingness of heart and a depth of love. When Jesus "went to work on his disciples", He was teaching them and demonstrating to them that servanthood isn't about self-help but rather self-sacrifice. He told them that self-sacrifice was the way to finding your true self and it is His way. Allowing another person or situation to dictate your life is counterintuitive in today's society. In fact, self-help has become the number one video status, book ranking and even attendance bringer. People are struggling in life and looking for answers but turning to those who teach self-help over servanthood. Jesus said self-help is no help at all. Does this mean we shouldn't try to get our bodies healthier or our brain in gear? No. It means that trying to muddle our way through our problems without Him is only causing muddy waters and quicksand situations. We are getting stuck in our own messes and finding that we cannot get out of the self-help mess we created. Jesus said that anyone who intends to come with Him has to let Him lead! He says for us to embrace the suffering and realize that He is in the driver's seat. This is not an easy thing and He tells us that He will show us how. No one likes uncomfortable situations. No one. No one enjoys suffering or pain. We as selfish people prefer indulgences. We want the best and are often willing to sacrifice things of God for things of fleshly indulgence. I remember teaching my boys to drive. Wes wasn't really into letting them in the driver's seat so that task fell to me. The hours of biting my lips and tongue to not say what I wanted to say have left my tongue permanently bruised but I will admit that John as the eldest got more direct instruction and overcorrection as Gabe was in the backseat and picked it up more easily.

He knew by the time it was his turn what I would lose it over and was a much more cautious driver. John was so excited to be in charge that he saw no "other driver" issues and drove as if he was the only one on the road, At first. His overconfidence in his own ability was the subject of many conversations until he began to see and learn. He knows now from lots of experiences just how irresponsible and irrational others can be but initially that wasn't the case. Learning at the feet of Jesus is an important lesson. Learning through His viewpoint and His perspective changes things beyond the moment. It allows us to look beyond our own abilities to see what He sees in us and in those around us. What kind of deal is it if you win in the moment but lose out in eternity? What is worth losing out on the eternal? I have watched many a person spend all they have on the pleasure of a moment, from alcohol induced fogs causing them to make poor choices to overall self-indulgent poor decisions such as drinking in the first place. When I was first teaching, I remember a sweet young man, whose mom I taught with, as he got his first car. He was so excited that he couldn't wait to show off. He drove off after school as his mom instructed him to go straight home and while on that journey home, he saw some kids from school running down the road. He saw them waving at him so he stopped the car and they got in. Hours later, the police showed up at his house and arrested him for being the getaway driver in a bank robbery and he went to jail. He chose to ignore the advice of his mother in a moment of self-indulgence and it cost him his freedom for many years.

Choices have consequences and we must recognize that we often cannot see down that road but God can. This is why we must take time to seek His will and listen to His ways. What is worth losing our soul for? That job? That boat? That hobby? That deer? That business? That person? What are we putting before God? Sacrifice isn't about oh, poor me. It is about taking the willing choice to put God first and be the servant He has called us to be. It is serving in His authority and power but also in the places of meeting needs. This can mean volunteering to serve as a nursery worker, children's church, serving the homeless, or a variety of other things but it can also mean putting our own dreams and plans on hold as we wait for His direction.

He says, "Follow me and I will show you how."

By entering through faith into what God has always wanted to do for us—set us right with him, make us fit for him—we have it all together with God because of our Master Jesus. And that's not all: We throw open our doors to God and discover at the same moment that he has already thrown open his door to us. We find ourselves standing where we always hoped we might stand—out in the wide open spaces of God's grace and glory, standing tall and shouting our praise.

Romans 5: 1-2

Wide, Open Spaces!

When my boys were in their tween years and we would stay at a hotel, we got adjoining rooms where there was a door in the room that opened into the other but it required the door to be opened on both sides. Gabriel loved to have the power of the door. He enjoyed getting to open and close his side knowing that our side was open almost like the game peek-a-boo you play with babies. Wes decided to play along and close our side as he could hear him opening and closing the door on his side. The game ensued with Gabriel knocking and Wes opening etc. When I read this scripture, I couldn't help picturing that same joy in our lives of throwing open the door to God realizing that He has already opened His door to us. Jesus came so that the door to eternal Life would always be open for us. He is the way, truth and life. When we choose to enter through the door by faith in Him, we realize He made the way for us and we find ourselves standing in the presence of the Almighty in the wide, open spaces of grace and glory...then we don't shout peek-a-boo but rather Hallelujah because He has overcome and left the doorway to eternal life open to all who will walk through. Jesus stands in His open doorway knocking at our adjoining door asking for us to join Him but it is our choice to open that doorway of faith and walk through into His presence. He has done the work, planned all and performed the tasks that set us right before God. He stands at the door awaiting our entrance into the place He prepared for us and paid the price for entry. It is completely up to us to enter fully into the room or keep playing the games at the door. One day soon, Jesus will come again to take His bride away and at that moment, the door will close unexpectedly on His side and the game will be over. It was time for dinner and Wes closed and locked the adjoining door. He told the boys it was time but they were so busy having fun that they didn't listen. We walked out of our room and to the main doorway. We knocked and John opened the door to a very upset Gabriel standing at the adjoining door crying. He ran to us and said I thought you left me because you closed the door and wouldn't answer. One day, sadly, there will be those who played the game and failed to heed the call. We have a choice and the time is now to walk through into His grace and glory before the door is closed. It is time.

David blessed God in full view of the entire congregation:
Blessed are you, God of Israel,
our father from of old and forever.
To you, O God, belong the greatness and the might, the glory, the victory, the majesty, the splendor; Yes! Everything in heaven, everything on earth; the kingdom all yours! You've raised yourself high over all. Riches and glory come from you, you're ruler over all; You hold strength and power in the palm of your hand to build up and strengthen all. And here we are, O God, our God, giving thanks to you, praising your splendid Name.

1 Chronicles 29: 10-13

In Full View!

I love how God does things in secret but I really love it when He does it in full view for His glory! Secret blessings are special but those that bless all are amazing and transformative. Jesus was crucified in full view, lifted up on a cross on a hill so no one could miss it just like the prophecy stated. It wasn't a sacrifice done in secret nor left for only a few but a full view offering for all who choose to accept it. David blessed God in full view of the entire kingdom. Why are we so secretive about our worship? Why is it something to be hidden or relegated to only a part of our lives that we keep hidden like a light under a shade? Jesus said to let our light shine so ALL may see it and glorify the Father! We are to proclaim His works and His miracles. We are to testify to His greatness. God is a God of miracles so why do we not shout it out rather than play it down? He is an awesome God! Lately I have seen more talk about the weather than the God who controls the storms and winds. God is our forever father. All glory, majesty, greatness, victory and splendor come from Him and are due to Him. Everything in Heaven and Earth is His. He has raised Himself over all and riches and glory are His. Strength and power are His. He has the ability to build up and strengthen all in His pinkie but yet we stumble when talking about Him. Great and mighty is the Lord our God. It is time that we begin to worship and proclaim His majesty in full view of our audiences. There is never a time to be ashamed of Him or who He is. Note that this passage of David blessing God comes from a heart filled from giving! Yes, giving not receiving! David had just given all His wealth and possessions to the building of the House of God and installed his son, Solomon as king. David is no longer the richest and most powerful king but his praise and blessings come from a heart of giving. If we cannot find a blessing in ourselves to give, then we start at the place of giving. For in giving, our hearts are opened to our blessings. We begin to see the storehouse of God as we give. A window of Heaven opens up and we begin to see His mercy and grace, His forgiveness and His blessings upon us. We begin to have a heart full of thankfulness and gratitude which changes our attitude into a place of blessings. Water is attracted to water. Blessing is attracted to giving. By blessing God, we open His storehouse of blessing upon our own lives and those around us. It starts with giving. Give out of a full heart even if your supply is weak. Give out of a grateful spirit even if you are in need. Give out of a pure countenance even if your heart is heavy, for God sees the cheerful giver and He sees the downtrodden. He sees us as we are and He is moved by our needs and our willingness to give in full view. Full view blessing doesn't mean we need to advertise on social media or the local gossip chain that we have but rather that we leave the blessings of God in full view. God sees our gift of sacrifice of self. Challenge yourself to throw open those windows and begin to bless God in full view. Quit hiding behind the "excuses" and begin to be the person who worships openly and fully in blessing the Creator. He cannot help but be delighted and excited by us when we delight in Him!

There's more: God's Word warns us of danger
and directs us to hidden treasure.
Otherwise how will we find our way?
Or know when we play the fool?
Clean the slate, God,
so we can start the day fresh!
Keep me from stupid sins,
from thinking I can take over your work;
Then I can start this day sun-washed,
scrubbed clean of the grime of sin.
These are the words in my mouth;
these are what I chew on and pray.
Accept them when I place them
on the morning altar,
O God, my Altar-Rock,
God, Priest-of-My-Altar.

Psalms 19: 11-14

Chew and Pray!

What are you chewing on? I am a gum chewer for fresh breath and because it allows me to think. I enjoy when the gum is a neuro gum full of vitamins for my brain but the flavor is short-lived making me spit it out pretty quickly unlike some gums that give long lasting flavor. God's word is a long lasting, full flavored, chewy type of offering. David says it warns us of danger and directs us to hidden treasure. His word is powerful, slate cleaning and freshening for our palate. I remember the first time I took students to a fancy French dinner and they misunderstood the purpose of the palate cleanser and thought it was a dish of ice cream. Their slate was cleaned in a big way! Some of us truly need a big scrubbing to erase the grime and grit of sin off so that we can start today in a fresh Son washed day with our minds set on the tasks He has set before us. How easy it is to get bogged down into the never enough, the stupid sins of trying to take over God's job. We have the map that tells us where the treasure is, how to get there, where the dangers are located and we even have a Spirit guide to take us along the path and yet so often we decide that we should try our hand at rewriting the path on the map even though we have no idea how to get there! There is a saying for this called "the blind leading the blind" meaning that when we cannot see, we cannot direct very well. We get so caught up in our own ways that we fail to realize we are trying to follow a map of our own making rather than His. It's about the treasure. In Matthew, Scripture tells us that where our treasure is, that is where our heart will be. In other words, our treasure directs our heart and if we set our treasure up in Heaven where neither moth, nor rust nor thieves can take it, then our heart will go along the path towards that treasure but if we aim for worldly treasure in terms of career or fame or fortune, then our heart will follow that path strewn with letdowns and disappointment. How do we find our way without playing the fool? Only with a pure heart set towards the treasure of Heaven as our eternity. Chew on this as it is full of flavor and very long lasting: God Himself has prepared a path for us that is perfect and leads to enormous rewards. The best treasure anyone could ever dream of awaits those who aim their hearts toward His Son. He said that He goes before us to prepare a place, that where He is, there we can be also. This is Jesus clearing the path of dangerous rocks and ruts, smoothing the road, paving it with gold so it is easy to find and impossible to miss but we must aim in that direction. The only way to get on that path towards Him is to put our hearts towards it by choosing to place our treasure in His capable hands. As we start this morning, we need to place our hopes and dreams upon the altar of the Rock. His word never fails, His love endures always and He is our High Priest where our help comes from in all things. Keep chewing...the flavor never fails...pray and chew....think on it...He didn't bring us this far to leave us. He didn't teach us His promises to let us down.

No test or temptation that comes your way is beyond the course of what others have had to face. All you need to remember is that God will never let you down; he'll never let you be pushed past your limit; he'll always be there to help you come through it.
1 Corinthians 10:13

Beyond the Limit!

Oftentimes we feel like God is pushing us or allowing things in our lives that are more than we can take but most of the time these are the opportunities for us to make our needs known to God, because the stretching is the place of growth. As a brain trainer, I understand that being pushed to the limit is stressful but it is also the sweet place of learning and growth. In Corinthians we are promised that God will not give us too much to bear in temptations and tests as He prepares a way of escape or rescue for us but we must know to cry out and declare that we need help. I can easily and truthfully say that I often stretch the speed limit. I have a heavy foot and often I push the limits or boundary because it is a great suggestion but I believe I can handle the faster speed. We are often like this with God too. We push and push to get our way even though He knows what is best for us and has set boundaries and limits. He knows that the path ahead is curved and at the speed we are going, we will not be able to manage the twists and turns so He sends warnings and road blocks or bumps to slow us down to His recommendation so that we will not be shaken or lost in an accident of our own making. Life's journey is not about the quickness of completion in this race but rather the connection with Him and those around us for His glory. It's not about rushing to retirement so we can finally enjoy life but the celebration of life daily. I love these flowers in this photo for they have a cute face when they bloom that looks like a little kid wearing a hat and they remind me that God wants me to stop and smell the roses in life and spend time in the Garden with Him. He is always there waiting on me to quit rushing around and breathe Him in. Look around and realize that many others have it worse than you and need you to be the one who slows down to take the time to point the way to a rest stop and a place of safety in Him.

When you are in a trial or temptation, feeling desperate and overwhelmed...stop at the rest stop of His word. Begin to praise Him and count the true blessings that are there in your life. Then and only then will you see He is there with you. When you are rushing through and stressed with life, you see things in a blur and unclearly, not recognizing Him in the stillness or in the moment. But if you slow down and take the time, you will hear Him in the music of the melody in your heart through the pain and struggle. You will see Him in those around you and feel his hands extended to you through others. You will notice Him in the quiet whispering to you that it will all be okay because He has it all planned out. Be still and know that He is God. We are okay no matter what it feels like right now because He is taking us through whatever we are going through in His way and His timing. Breathe. See the flowers that never worry because they know the rain will come but they also know the sun will shine again. All we have to remember is that God will never let us down. It may not be in our time nor in our plan but He has the perfect spouse, the perfect situations, the perfect home, the perfect future... He has it all in His time. Breathe and trust that nothing is beyond His limits for He is beyond what our finite mind can comprehend and He will take us beyond our limits with Him to stretch us but never past what we can bear with Him! Time to go stretch in prayer so our limits can be boosted!

Celebrate God all day, every day. I mean, revel in him! Make it as clear as you can to all you meet that you're on their side, working with them and not against them. Help them see that the Master is about to arrive.
He could show up any minute!
Don't fret or worry. Instead of worrying, pray. Let petitions and praises shape your worries into prayers, letting God know your concerns. Before you know it, a sense of God's wholeness, everything coming together for good, will come and settle you down. It's wonderful what happens when Christ displaces worry at the center of your life.

Philipians 4: 4-7

Displace Worry!

I don't know about y'all but I'm a party girl! I don't bar hop or drink but I like celebrating things and people! I cannot stand negativity and worry. Fear is not my cup of tea either. I love celebrating life and God's goodness. I like to start my day celebrating God with my music up loud and my prayers louder. I like to dance around in the Spirit and cheer God but some days it is hard. Somedays, pain or weakness, frustration or sorrow takes our breath and the celebration is hard to find. This is when it is even more important and we may have to dig deep. This is why He tells us to fellowship with other believers. It isn't just about the corporate worship on Sunday although that can be the tone setter for your week...it is about the cheerleading during the tough times. It is about making others see that we're all in this battle of life together but God is in control and He has already won. When we are weary or hurting, it is then we can truly recognize the need for another to lift us up. When we are not down, it's our turn to be the lifter. I cheered a little in college, not because I was a skinny mini or anything but because I was willing to encourage others. Sometimes I was the person who was lifting another up and sometimes I was the person being lifted. Cheering is a skill that requires digging deep and finding a sense of hope and excitement even when things don't look good as well as when they are amazing! It is easy to celebrate and revel when you are on the winning team and we must remember that with God we are always on the winning team even when it doesn't look that way. In Philippians, we are instructed to let our petitions for what we need and our praises be shaped into prayers. The only way to do this is by reshaping what seems negative or hopeless with promises and blessings recounted. Sometimes we are the encourager and sometimes we need the encouragement. This is the purpose of a team of believers who pull together. There is one specific person I have in my life who always gets me back up and seems to know when I am down without me voicing it. She sends me hilarious creature photos, texts and cards. They make me laugh and smile in hard times. This is the purpose of the body of Christ! She has every reason to whine and complain but I have never seen her do it. She melts the cold weight of life with her joy!

This photo is a picture of trees covered in ice. It is beautiful to see but I promise you it isn't a fun experience for the tree. The weight breaks branches and the cold traumatizes the tree and it causes many trees to even die. But the ice sparkling in the sunlight creates a beautiful photo of His creation even in the circumstances of dire straits. We need to Think of this next time our burden is weighing us down and straighten our crowns. The sparkling diamonds of cold hard stress that are seemingly breaking us down are really opportunistic times to cheer and sparkle in His Sonshine. We have to get our perspective straight so we can realize that the Master is on His way. Shout to the Lord. Let Him know whatsoever we desire to share and in His praises comes a sense of wholeness and rightness. Jesus at the center of it all displaces worry and turns the weight into water. The sun melts the ice turning it into the water that feeds the tree allowing it to grow. Allow the Sonshine of His praise to melt the weight of the icy worry and stress in our lives turning it into blessings instead that feed and nurture our souls. Shout to the Lord! Declare His mightiness! Scream and cheer! He has won and we are on His team! Celebrate Jesus!

But you, dear friends, carefully build yourselves up in this most holy faith by praying in the Holy Spirit, staying right at the center of God's love, keeping your arms open and outstretched, ready for the mercy of our Master, Jesus Christ. This is the unending life, the real life!

Go easy on those who hesitate in the faith. Go after those who take the wrong way. Be tender with sinners, but not soft on sin. The sin itself stinks to high heaven.

And now to him who can keep you on your feet, standing tall in his bright presence, fresh and celebrating—to our one God, our only Savior, through Jesus Christ, our Master, be glory, majesty, strength, and rule before all time, and now, and to the end of all time. Yes.

Jude 1: 20-25

Centered!

Reading the book of Jude is easy and profound at the same time because one chapter covers so much ground. In 25 short verses, he reminds us to relax that God has it all in control, helps us refocus our thoughts and challenges us to remember who God is while not being distracted by those who are false. As he ends the letter, he gives us the most important thing to target-the center. Jesus is the center of it all. I think it is safe to say that there is a lot of disgusting behavior and disappointment in leaders in our world. Standards of living and morals have degraded so far that many people do not even know who they are and are left wandering, making foolish choices, completely wayward and so lost. In Matthew, he says that Jesus looked out over the lost and was brokenhearted by their complete lostness. Like Him, I look around me and see prophecy being fulfilled. Signs of the times are popping up everywhere and the biggest one is the complete loss of the center. Political talking heads taunt the right, the left, the moderate, the liberal, the conservative, the elephant and the donkey....the truth is that we have lost our center. Since having back surgery, my balance is precarious if I am not careful because my core is weak. A weak core makes for tough balance as the center of gravity can shift quickly tilting one over easily. The therapists all recommend exercise to rebuild the core muscles so that's what I do daily. I have to deliberately focus on rebuilding my core center of gravity. When something starts spinning, as long as it has a center of focus that is consistent and anchored, it will spin equally and stay centered but the minute the core is affected or becomes untethered, instability is introduced which will lead ultimately to destruction of either the things around it or the thing itself but most likely both. Staying in the center of God's love while keeping our arms open and outstretched for the mercy of Jesus is how we keep our balance in this spinning world of lies and deception. Staying centered requires building our core up in the faith by praying through the Holy Spirit and diving deep into His word. Jude also instructs us that when we have found our balance, we are to be patient with those who are still trying to find theirs and those who hesitate in faith as well as to go after those who are spinning out of control. Offer our hand in friendship and love, embrace them but not their sin. I think of my babies as they learned to walk. They teetered and tottered but they would stretch their hands out for balance. At first, they wanted my hands to help, then they wanted to do it alone but would get frustrated with me when they fell because I didn't catch them. Often as I grabbed them, I would realize that their core had shifted causing them to fall because they had a dirty diaper. As I embraced that baby in love, I embarked on removing that nasty smelling diaper and disposing of it quickly. I didn't embrace that stinky thing...even though I loved the child who had dirtied that diaper. God centers us, cleans us, sets us apart and is there for us through all just like the loving parent. When we get out of sorts, refusing His guidance and causing disruption to our core which makes us stumble and fall, He is there to change us and make us new but we must be willing to get recentered in Him. It is time for us to shake off the heavy sins, lift out our hands for His mercy and allow Him to rebalance our lives in the center of it all. He keeps us on our feet, standing, talking in His presence, fresh and clean from the weighty, stinky sin so we May celebrate our God through Jesus for His majesty, strength, glory and rule for all of time.

So let's do it—full of belief, confident that we're presentable inside and out. Let's keep a firm grip on the promises that keep us going. He always keeps his word. Let's see how inventive we can be in encouraging love and helping out, not avoiding worshiping together as some do but spurring each other on, especially as we see the big Day approaching.

Hebrews 10: 22-25

Spurred On!

One of my favorite people in the world races on her horse and does amazing things on horseback but that horse must become one with her to be motivated and learn the signals to do what she instructs. It takes a team of people supporting her to get her from place to place with her horse and lots of coordination but it is done in love by her family because they see her passion and desire to be encouraging to her which motivates her to do better and more. God tells us to gather together to spur each other on. What this means is to motivate one another to the next place of moving forward in Him. Years ago when I was teaching, my principal took us to this thing called a Ropes course which was a popular thing back then to encourage camaraderie and pulling together. In the course you are given a task of getting everyone from point A to point C via point B but only two persons can be at Point B at one time and that was a tight fit. We had to work together to move each other and motivate each other because...Point A was on the ground...point B was a light pole in the middle-yea, a literal light pole high in the air..and point C was the place/cabin we were meeting. The only way up was through this pulley system which required people moving it. Needless to say, it was quite the accomplishment when we made it to the cabin at the top and boy did we feel good until we discovered that the only way down was the same system. The challenges of those who had to overcome health issues, fear of heights and small places, and other things, was enormous. (I think they had to stop these because of lawsuits or lack of people willing to commit). The point is that the only way to accomplish the task was together, spurring each other on and cheering, encouraging, promising, cajoling...it was a lot of work but so worth it when done as we were a tighter group and learned a lot about one another out of necessity. The devil wants to isolate us, commercialize us, limit our effectiveness by making us look at our own situation constantly and our future plans with trepidation not realizing that God has not given us a spirit of fear but of love & a sound mind. He has also given us a great cloud of witnesses and a family of believers who stand with us when our situation seems impossible. These are those who are our people movers, motivators, prayer warriors, intercessors, confidantes, promise keepers and cheerleaders or encouragers. They can be family by earthly blood and/or family by Christ's blood. This is our confidence, that we who are full of belief can know that we are presentable to Christ by keeping a firm grip on the promises of God that keep us going. He always keeps His word. We are challenged to be inventive or creative in how we encourage love and help others out in our gathering of worship and spurring each other on especially as the day draws near of Jesus' return. Signs of the times are everywhere. People are neglecting the truth and wandering further away from the light because it has been there so long they think it will always be there. We are in a dark cave walking in the Light shining and we see those around us wandering off the path out of frustration or lack of encouragement...our job is to get all of our community around us into the Light. Our job isn't to tear down another church or group who is preaching Jesus no matter if we agree with their method or not. Our job is to get all of our family into the path by inventive means. We are to help them to see Who He is and Where the Light is and Why we are on this path then encourage them to join us, stay the course and continue forward. It's not about your career-that's the marketplace of ministry to others God gave you but that is not your final destination. It isn't about your marriage, your home, your church, your life...it is about Him and how much closer to Him and Heaven you are becoming. Let's spur one another on. A spurring is more than cheering. You see a spur to a horse has a little dig, not permanent pain but a momentary reminder of who the boss is in the experience of riding. We are a team of horses headed to the destination and sometimes the spurring rider (Jesus) must dig in and remind us that He is God and the Chief in charge. We can see the spurring of others and watch those who have made it home with encouragement knowing that we are here just a little while until we achieve the ultimate goal of our Heavenly Home. Who can you spur on today? Can you dig a little in the love of God and bless someone into memory of who He is? Can you speak a Godly truth in love into the life of another? Can you pray or bless someone with a special something to remind them that God loves them and we are on this journey together? A phone call? A card? A gift? A post? A text? Can you find a way to spur or cheer someone closer to the goal today? Let's be inventive with our incentives because Jesus is coming! The Light came into this world and His own received Him not, so as many as are called to His purpose, He invites you to the wedding supper of the bride which He has prepared in honor of the Bridegroom-Jesus...

The old plan was only a hint of the good things in the new plan. Since that old "law plan" wasn't complete in itself, it couldn't complete those who followed it. No matter how many sacrifices were offered year after year, they never added up to a complete solution. If they had, the worshipers would have gone blissfully on their way, no longer dragged down by their sins. But instead of removing awareness of sin, when those animal sacrifices were repeated over and over they actually heightened awareness and guilt. The plain fact is that bull and goat blood can't get rid of sin. That is what is meant by this prophecy, put in the mouth of Christ:
You don't want sacrifices and offerings year after year; you've prepared a body for me for a sacrifice. It's not fragrance and smoke from the altar that whet your appetite. So I said, "I'm here to do it your way, O God, the way it's described in your Book."
When he said, "You don't want sacrifices and offerings," he was referring to practices according to the old plan. When he added, "I'm here to do it your way," he set aside the first in order to enact the new plan–God's way–by which we are made fit for God by the once-for-all sacrifice of Jesus.

Hebrews 10: 1-10

Once and For All!

I will say that the smoke and fragrance from Wes' pork whetted my appetite for lunch but that is not my motivation to go to church. My motivation comes from "The Once and For All". Fairytales and such start with a Once Upon a Time to tell a story of love, danger, romance, warriors, conquest, etc. but God chose to tell a story of Once and For All. Once Upon a Time, God sent His son on the ultimate journey of conquest to share His love with a wayward group of people but that story was not completed with a "The End", for the sacrifice He made was a Once and For All tale which becomes a reality for each of us as we step into His story of love. The fact is that there is nothing for us to do to be a part of the story except to accept His love for us. The story of love was already written and we get to be the winning princes and princesses who are saved from the dragon of sin and the fiery pit of hell by the perfect knight/savior on a white horse declaring victory. His sacrifice of His life once and for all met all the demands of the word and He who was the King of Kings became the Prince of Peace, the Mighty Counselor and the Lion of Judah all by choosing to take the role of the Lamb of God who took on the sin of the world. When He chose to take on the role of Savior to all mankind, He enacted the new plan setting aside the first order by meeting all the obstacles head on. He chose to do it God's way. His book is full of stories of conquest and triumph but none match the story of love. What love, that this God would choose to send His only son as a sacrifice of atonement for us to demonstrate His powerful commitment to us that while we were yet unknown to ourselves, He gave once and for all. The Once upon a time became The Once and For All through His willingness to say "I'm here God to do it your way." The ending to this story is still playing out. We have a choice to succumb to the fiery pit of hell with the beastly dragon of sin pulling us into his lair or to open our arms and our hearts by simply repeating the phrase that Jesus said. Then our Once and For All Savior will snatch us from the clutches of the beast and bring us into His glorious Heavenly home full of riches and wonders to be in the place of honor with Him. Let's say it.... I'm here God to do it your way. I accept your gift of Once and for all! I choose to be a part of your story told your way Once and for all time!

"Quiet down, far-flung ocean islands. Listen!
Sit down and rest, everyone. Recover your strength.
Gather around me. Say what's on your heart.
Together let's decide what's right.

Isaiah 41: 1

Together!

Exhausted? Frustrated? Discouraged? Forlorn? Tired of chasing rainbows? Tired of being spun and twirled by life's ups and downs? Isaiah proclaims for us to quiet down and quit being volcanic in our lives spewing and sputtering the yuck from inside us onto those around us and burning them alive. Time to Sit down, rest and recover our strength at Jesus' feet. He says to gather around Him and say what's on our hearts then together we will decide on what's right. There is such peace in that. We can not decide together until we gather around Him. As long as we are far flung islands unto ourselves spewing and sputtering about what's not right and not happening and throwing up our frustration onto others, we are lonely and confused, hurting ourselves and those around us. Often we get so overwhelmed with our wanting that we fail to see our blessings. We get so caught up in the grass is greener mindset that we fail to see the beauty at our feet. Listen! Sit down! Rest! Recover! Gather with Jesus and share all your troubles.

Together means in close companionship. We cannot be in close companionship with anyone unless we spend time getting to know them and stay in close relationship with them. I have watched relationships fail time after time because the people in the relationship grew apart as they changed throughout time and they didn't spend time together. They existed in a solo plane and when the engine failed they crashed because they didn't take the time to do maintenance and care for the relationship. Together means that one side is not dictating things but that the persons are in agreement. Often, we look at God as this being, directing our lives and orchestrating it beyond our control, but when I look at scripture, I see time after time that God's hand was moved by a man, a prayer, and a together moment. Joshua commanded the sun to stand still and God did it. Paul commanded a man to walk who was lame and God healed him in the name of Jesus. God's authority was given to us through Jesus when we are aligned with Him. That's the way-together. Close alignment of two magnets is so powerful that you can feel the attraction between them. They are drawn together by an invisible force because they're alignment to be one is so powerful. This is the kind of togetherness God wants with us. In the beginning, in the cool of the evening, God walked with Adam. God desires togetherness. Jesus called disciples to walk with Him during His time here on Earth. Listen! Grab this! God wants us to be together with Him. He wants us to come to Him and chat! He wants us to be closer to Him than any other but that relationship takes time, effort and work to maintain. We must spend time in His presence. We must take time to rest, recover and dwell with Him in refreshing and say what's on our hearts. Put the phone down, turn the tv off, get away with Him in nature or a quiet place and recover the truth of who He is. Quit spewing and start listening! He desires us to be all we want to be but first we must know who we are in Him. Together.

All those wants, dreams and desires can be resolved if we gather together with Him.

Jesus said, "Why do you question me about what's good? God is the One who is good. If you want to enter the life of God, just do what he tells you."

As he watched him go, Jesus told his disciples, "Do you have any idea how difficult it is for the rich to enter God's kingdom? Let me tell you, it's easier to gallop a camel through a needle's eye than for the rich to enter God's kingdom."

The disciples were staggered.

"Then who has any chance at all?"

Jesus looked hard at them and said, "No chance at all if you think you can pull it off yourself. Every chance in the world if you trust God to do it."

Matthew 19: 17, 23-26

Chances!

I have never played the lottery or gambled though I know many do chance their money on such for the maybe. Lately, even investing is a little like gambling because it is so uncertain as are most things now. I have always been more inclined to invest in what I know is certain or has good ROI (return on investment). I have invested my life into that which lays up treasures where neither rust nor moth can destroy it. I choose to invest in people and in the kingdom of God. In Matthew, a rich young man came to Jesus asking how to get to Heaven and Jesus told him to follow the commandments. He assured Jesus that he had done so living a good life, then Jesus told him that if he truly wanted all of Heaven's offerings he should sell all he owned and give it to the poor then follow Jesus. As he walked away downcast, Jesus spoke to his disciples about how hard it is for a rich man or woman to enter Heaven; Not because of the riches but because they love money more than God. Richness or wealth alone does not make us more likely to miss Heaven but the love of things over God does. Wealth and status has always been a sign of power and ability but Jesus was stating that the values of this world are not the values of God. This blew the disciples minds, especially Judas who had already begun to value money over God Himself in the flesh. What Jesus was saying wasn't strictly about wealth but about riches. Where the treasure of the heart is where we invest our lives, purpose and being. Jesus said there is no chance of any of us entering Heaven if we think we can do it. It isn't about us, it is about Him. See, that rich young man had a chance to invest all he had into the kingdom and spend quality time with Jesus but he was so used to having it his way-a life of ease that when he looked at their lifestyle, he wasn't willing to sacrifice his ease. Living a life of trust over a life of surety in the world's economy is hard. It is a life that requires pressing in and faith as opposed to a confidence in what seems more certain. A poor man has no risk in investing in the kingdom for he has only hope to hold onto but a rich man holds tight to his wealth and believes in his authority through it. I am not against having money.

Money is a good thing to have and it is necessary to pay bills. I am not against richness, wealth, fame or anything associated unless it diminishes the kingdom of God. Recently a person I know won a large amount and it changed them from a person of giving to a person of hoarding. I watched this person become someone else as they lavishly spent on themselves and no longer invested in people. I was shocked. I thought I knew her but now she has riches and that changed who she was. This is what Jesus is warning us of in scripture. It is the "I can do it my way" mentality that comes from riches, fame, indulgence and being spoiled. Most of us are more self indulgent than we think. A friend told me recently that I was a hard person to get a gift for because I could get whatever I wanted. I was hurt at first until I realized that this is often the truth about all of us. We are blessed. We rarely do without. We are not used to sacrificing but if we do, it is only for a bit. In terms of the world, we are all "the rich person", who is "the camel", trying to go through "the eye of the needle". In many countries, the average salary per year is under $50. Yes, that's the amount we spend on an outfit or shoes or a meal when in other countries, that amount feeds and cares for a family for a year. Here's a test. What if I told you to just give up your Starbucks coffee or whatever special drink/food you love for one month and put that money you would've spent into an empty coffee cup and pray over it. Then at the end of the month, donate it to missions so that someone can go tell others about Jesus. Could you do it? This is what Jesus is saying about wealth. It leads to self indulgence so much that we cannot sacrifice our desires. We make excuses and say well I already give enough. This is the mindset that Jesus says is dangerous because it isn't about faith or trust or hope but about ME! If you want to enter the life of God, just do what He tells you to do. Listen! I know that this is taking a chance but this gamble is a surety. It has guaranteed return on investment. Take that money you're planning to spend on the lottery and invest it into the offering plate instead where the return is laid up in Heaven and the government doesn't get 20%...in fact, you actually get a savings or deductible off taxes for investors in the kingdom of God. Invest yourself, time, money, talents into Him because there is every chance in the world you will go to Heaven and reign with Him if you invest faithfully in Him.

The powerball is being called, just do what He says.

Consider it a sheer gift, friends, when tests and challenges come at you from all sides. You know that under pressure, your faith-life is forced into the open and shows its true colors. So don't try to get out of anything prematurely. Let it do its work so you become mature and well-developed, not deficient in any way. If you don't know what you're doing, pray to the Father. He loves to help. You'll get his help, and won't be condescended to when you ask for it. Ask boldly, believingly, without a second thought. People who "worry their prayers" are like wind-whipped waves. Don't think you're going to get anything from the Master that way, adrift at sea, keeping all your options open.

When down-and-outers get a break, cheer! And when the arrogant rich are brought down to size, cheer! Prosperity is as short-lived as a wildflower, so don't ever count on it. You know that as soon as the sun rises, pouring down its scorching heat, the flower withers. Its petals wilt and, before you know it, that beautiful face is a barren stem. Well, that's a picture of the "prosperous life." At the very moment everyone is looking on in admiration, it fades away to nothing. Anyone who meets a testing challenge head-on and manages to stick it out is mighty fortunate. For such persons loyally in love with God, the reward is life and more life.

Don't let anyone under pressure to give in to evil say, "God is trying to trip me up." God is impervious to evil, and puts evil in no one's way. The temptation to give in to evil comes from us and only us. We have no one to blame but the leering, seducing flare-up of our own lust. Lust gets pregnant, and has a baby: sin! Sin grows up to adulthood, and becomes a real killer.

So, my very dear friends, don't get thrown off course. Every desirable and beneficial gift comes out of heaven. The gifts are rivers of light cascading down from the Father of Light. There is nothing deceitful in God, nothing two-faced, nothing fickle. He brought us to life using the true Word, showing us off as the crown of all his creatures.

James 1: 2-18

Diamond Teardrops!

After loss of a child...How to go on when you don't want to live...Hurting & healing! Only His words. No others will do! Attitude of Gratitude Giving thanks through the hard times...counting it all joy.

"Consider it a sheer gift, friends, when tests and challenges come at you from all sides. You know that under pressure, your faith-life is forced into the open and shows its true colors. So don't try to get out of anything prematurely. Let it do its work so you become mature and well-developed, not deficient in any way.

If you don't know what you're doing, pray to the Father. He loves to help. You'll get his help, and won't be condescended to when you ask for it. Ask boldly, believingly, without a second thought. People who "worry their prayers" are like wind-whipped waves. Don't think you're going to get anything from the Master that way, adrift at sea, keeping all your options open. When down-and-outers get a break, cheer! And when the arrogant rich are brought down to size, cheer! Prosperity is as short-lived as a wildflower, so don't ever count on it. You know that as soon as the sun rises, pouring down its scorching heat, the flower withers. Its petals wilt and, before you know it, that beautiful face is a barren stem. Well, that's a picture of the "prosperous life." At the very moment everyone is looking on in admiration, it fades away to nothing.

Anyone who meets a testing challenge head-on and manages to stick it out is mighty fortunate. For such persons loyally in love with God, the reward is life and more life. Don't let anyone under pressure to give in to evil say, "God is trying to trip me up." God is impervious to evil, and puts evil in no one's way. The temptation to give in to evil comes from us and only us. We have no one to blame but the leering, seducing flare-up of our own lust. Lust gets pregnant, and has a baby: sin! Sin grows up to adulthood, and becomes a real killer. So, my very dear friends, don't get thrown off course. Every desirable and beneficial gift comes out of heaven. The gifts are rivers of light cascading down from the Father of Light. There is nothing deceitful in God, nothing two-faced, nothing fickle. He brought us to life using the true Word, showing us off as the crown of all his creatures." James 1:2-18 MSG

Doing something for you, bringing
something to you—
that's not what you're after.
Being religious, acting pious—
that's not what you're asking for.
You've opened my ears
so I can listen.
So I answered, "I'm coming.
I read in your letter what
you wrote about me,
And I'm coming to the party
you're throwing for me."
That's when God's Word entered my life,
became part of my very being.

Psalms 40: 6-8

My Very Being!

GROWTH
God reared ownership with the Highest!
Greatness I can achieve
Reaching up to new heights
Only as I believe that through God
With effort, I can accomplish
These tasks I have set before me that
Help to make me who I am

God is throwing a party for me and everyone is invited! You can read what He wrote about me in His words of love recorded in His book. It's not about me! It's about you! It's your party too! I can tell you that as a business owner and a brain trainer, I love reading the stories of success my clients share because while those stories are about their accomplishments, they include me because I was a part of their story. I do not know a single parent or grandparent that doesn't light up from inside out when asked about their child. What do you love about your child? What makes them unique and special to you? These questions bring this drifty look of a dreamer gazing into the place of Heaven. Each of us is valued like this by God. He created us in the innermost being of our mother's womb and knows us intimately. He gets a dreamy look when asked about us. He loves us endlessly. Ask a grandparent about their grandchildren and out come the photos, the stories, the memories and the legacy. This is what David was writing about in this song. God is crazy about us! He wrote to you and me, about you and me, thinking about you and me before we were ever you and me. It isn't about religion or being pious that we know God and all His ways because we don't. That's not what He wants. He wants us. He desires time with us, to bless us, to cherish us, to spend time with us. He is proud of us just for being who He created. God's word enters into you and becomes a very part of your being when you embrace that He wants you just because you are you! He isn't about what you have or can do. He's not about your abilities or inabilities. He's not about your haves or lacks, your wants or even your needs. He's about you and me! He loves us! Oh, how He loves us! When we grasp His love for us and it takes root deep in us, He becomes our story. I love throwing parties for others. I like thinking about them and making a special moment to celebrate them because it fills me up with love and allows me to be a part of their story too through my celebration of them. Our love story of God is the party that He is throwing for us! I can picture the conversation as He talks with Jesus about me.

"Have you seen how Donesa loves others?"
"Well, of course, she got that from me."
"She is a favorite of mine because I love the time we spend together."
"Let me show you what she did today...can you believe that?"
"She called on me because she was feeling discouraged and I reminded her who I was!"
"Let's throw her a love party today in the sky"
"How about a rainbow? You know she really loves seeing those as they remind her of who we are."

Yes, these are my imaginary conversations that God has about me but He does you know! He thinks about me and you. He takes time to do things just for you and me. He is all about you and me. We are His purpose just as He is ours. When we truly grasp this, His word becomes a part of our very being just like the skin on our bodies but more. When His word enters our lives and takes root, it is like a party or celebration exploding with fireworks because we see how He wrote about us. His promises are our promises! His words are our authority! His rainbow is just for us-rivers of light cascading down from the Father of Light! What is He writing about us? Are we listening? Seeing? Walking? Believing? Let's get this party started!

He's coming and He's prepared it all for us! Grasp this and you'll walk a little taller and more confident today! When we focus on Him, we realize that He is focused on us! Quit getting bogged down by the naysayers! The God of the Universe is throwing a party for us in the best venue ever with streets of gold and gates of pearls. It is the hottest shindig around and everyone wants to attend. Better yet, He wrote a letter all about us. Get started reading it and you'll be amazed at how well He knows you and how much He has done to prepare a place for you!

Talk and act like a person expecting to be judged by the Rule that sets us free. For if you refuse to act kindly, you can hardly expect to be treated kindly. Kind mercy wins over harsh judgment every time.

Dear friends, do you think you'll get anywhere in this if you learn all the right words but never do anything? Does merely talking about faith indicate that a person really has it? For instance, you come upon an old friend dressed in rags and half-starved and say, "Good morning, friend! Be clothed in Christ! Be filled with the Holy Spirit!" and walk off without providing so much as a coat or a cup of soup—where does that get you? Isn't it obvious that God-talk without God-acts is outrageous nonsense?

James 2: 12-17

The Freedom Rule!

James 2 is a robust and real tough speaking chapter. He just gets out there telling it like it is. The rule of law is tough but the Rule of Freedom is tougher because it requires sacrifice. There is an old joke involving the difference of being involved or committed...it is about a pig and a hen walking down the road past a billboard with a picture of a ham/egg breakfast on it. The hen says she is happy to contribute and the pig says yes, for you it is only a donation but for me it is sacrifice. The Freedom Rule requires commitment not just being involved. It requires us to walk out our faith, not just talk about it. Recently I had a conversation about love with a friend. Love is a choice. Like a beautiful rose bush filled with flowers, it smells fragrant and blooms beautifully but it also has thorns, needs care and sometimes requires pruning. Love is a very complicated sacrifice of self. It is a choice that seems easy but when tough times come, we often have to choose to walk it out when it would be easier to just walk away. True faith that leads to freedom isn't about the talk but about the walk through the hard times. We are such fickle people by nature, selfish and self-indulgent to a fault. James reminds us that we should talk and act (walk) like we are being judged. I have a girlfriend who was a contestant in Miss America years ago and she still walks like that. So I asked her one day why she still practices that same walk and she told me that she chose to become that person who was a step above, always competing for the top because she was always becoming. "Becoming what?" I asked. "The woman I want to be", she responded. I look at her differently now. She hasn't settled. She sees her role in life as a constant place to move upward into the next place. Striving. That's the word. The Freedom Rule is that in this journey of life we walk in, Jesus has sacrificed for our freedom but we must walk in it. We must walk it out in those around us. James says it like this: God talk without God acts is nonsense. He goes on in chapter 2 to illustrate this through many of the stories recorded in scripture from Abraham to Rahab. God has given us freedom from the weight of sin but He has also charged us to take up the cross of Christ and follow Him. This requires us to walk out our faith in love with those around us whether they are thorny or fragrant. The thorns come before the flower blooms but the attraction and fragrance of the flower makes us often overlook the thorns until we reach out. Loving a prickly pear person is hard but the fruit is worth the sacrifice. As James says, Kind mercy wins over harsh judgment every time! You cannot expect kindness if you never give it. Who can we love through the thorns into God's kingdom today?

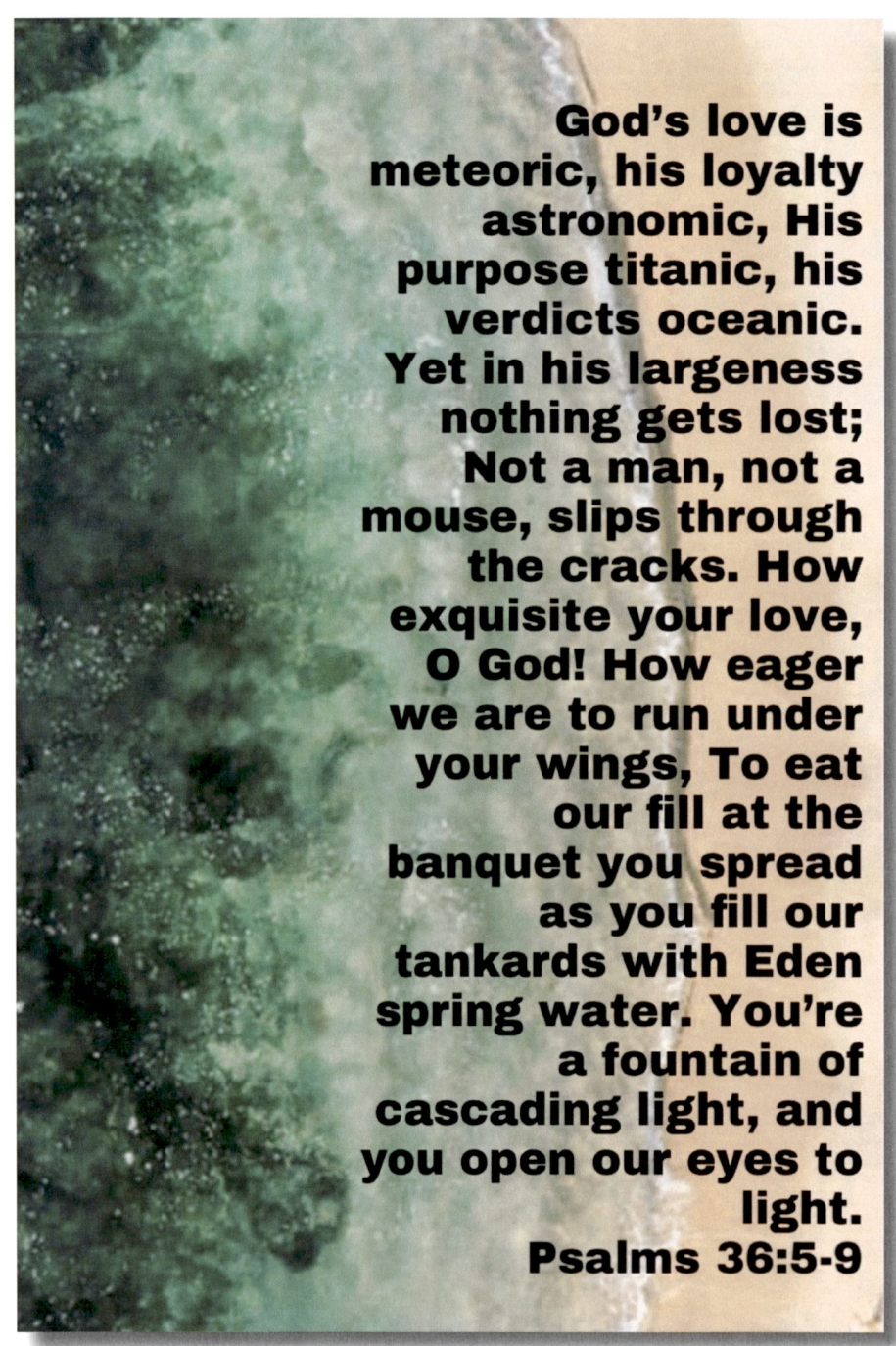

God's love is meteoric, his loyalty astronomic, His purpose titanic, his verdicts oceanic. Yet in his largeness nothing gets lost; Not a man, not a mouse, slips through the cracks. How exquisite your love, O God! How eager we are to run under your wings, To eat our fill at the banquet you spread as you fill our tankards with Eden spring water. You're a fountain of cascading light, and you open our eyes to light.
Psalms 36:5-9

Oceanic Verdicts!

Restoration you need invigorates you. I am saying this from a place of finally getting sorely needed rest last night. Last night I finally slept almost all night for the first time in ages. You see nothing gets lost with God. He knew I needed that rest desperately and allowed me to get it. God's love is so deep, so wide, so fathomless that we cannot measure it. It is like looking at the dawn as it begins. First we grasp a minute glimpse of light then gradually it increases until it explodes on the horizon in cascading light of all colors. The cool thing is that despite God's largeness of love and astronomic loyalty, nothing gets lost to Him. I mean I cannot keep up with things at my desk, much less my home. Sometimes I search for a while before I find what I am looking for in my home because I know it is there but cannot immediately locate it. God doesn't lose us. He doesn't misplace things either. Not a man nor a mouse is lost to Him. He intimately knows us, loves us, fills us and provides for us. I think this picture is exquisite. It is a photo of the beach with the emerald waters of His love pouring over the grains of sand and He knows each drop of water and each grain of sand as intimately as He knows us. The photo cannot capture the exquisite depths of His love for there is no way to capture it in that format but He made us a vessel to hold His love. How eager we are to run to Him to hide under His wings in our need and eat our fill of His provisions of wonder at His banquet of love. He gives us the waters of Eden (eternal life) as a quencher for our thirst. He provides what we need when we need it. When we look at all God is and all He has created, it boggles our minds that He also knows where each grain of sand is deposited. He knows that grain of sand that slipped into the oyster causing it pain and anguish just like He knows the things that slip into our lives causing the same. And just like the oyster was given the chemicals needed to cover that grain of sand in a coating of pearl, God has given us the tools to turn our sorriest things into pearls of great price through Him. He has provided a way where there seems no way. He has provided the banquet and the waters of life before we are even ready or in need. He knows our need for sleep, rest, relief and restoration. He knows that we are a struggling people with a tendency to turn to our own ways as the ocean roars towards the beach in waves. He knows each grain of sand that will be carried away in our lives and each drop of watery tears that will be shed and He cherishes it all for He knows us intimately and created us. Why are we getting down and discouraged? Only because we get our eyes off Him and begin to focus on the water around us instead of seeing that He controls the waves as He creates the tides. He is the ebb and flow that all of Earth attunes to in its rhythm. We too are tuned to who He is and only when we get out of sync do we start looking at other drops of water or grains of sand to save us rather than the Wave Walker. I know the peace speaker by name. Start to worship and our vessel of His making will fill with His wondrous love. This is how we make pearls from our grains of sand that cause our pain, sorrow and anguish.

Time to make a pearl!

For I consider that the sufferings of this present time are not worthy to be compared with the glory which shall be revealed in us.

Romans 8: 18

Pearl of Great Price!

"Did you know….An oyster that has not been wounded in any way does not produce pearls?"

A pearl is a healed wound.

Pearls are a product of pain, the result of a foreign or unwanted substance entering the oyster, such as a parasite or a grain of sand.

The inside of an oyster shell is a shiny substance called "nacre."

When a grain of sand enters, the nacre cells go to work and cover the grain of sand with layers and more layers to protect the defenseless body from the oyster. As a result, a beautiful pearl is formed!

The more pearls, the more valuable…

God never allows pain without a purpose.

What if your greatest ministry to others comes out of your greatest hurt or deepest wounds?

The hard things we may be going through now are really nothing in comparison to the glory that will be revealed in us later.
(Romans 8:17-18)

♡-author unknown

God's Decree!

Jeremiah 15:5-9

Are you in a place where blatant sin abounds? Does your heart break for them?

Spend some time today praying for the unrepentant souls and for revival in our land.

Key thought for today:

Empty Handed!

Isaiah 55:8-11

What are the tools that God has given you to use? Are you using them the way He intended you to?

Pray over your talent and let it be used by God.

Key thought for today:

Armloads of Blessings!

Psalms 126:4-6

Are you or someone you know dealing with a loss of hope? Be encouraged by God's word, He will bring blessings to those who call and wait upon Him!

Pray for God to send the "rain of joy" into your/their life.

Key thought for today:

The Greatest Myth!

Philippians 4:4-5

What are you anticipating and celebrating?

Are you making it clear in all your actions and deeds, words and abilities in this season that Christ is the message of Christmas?

Key thought for today:

Star Birth!

Daniel 12:1-3

What is our role in this life?

What kind of star will you be?

Key thought for today:

Climb Out of the Coffin!

Ephesians 5:11-16

Our days are filled with whirlwinds of activity, but which of these are truly of eternal value?

How can we live a pursuit of Godliness?

Key thought for today:

Sin Damaged!

1 John 4:7-10

Is your relationship with God where it should be or have you allowed busyness to grab all your attention?

Does your walk with God have you covered in "Love Spots"?

Key thought for today:

Son-burst Light!

Isaiah 9:2-7

Are you looking at the light and walking in the light or are you looking at the darkness while walking in the light?

Key thought for today:

Tackle Your Yard!

Matthew 10:5-8

What does your yard look like?

Where is your marketplace of ministry?

What are your actions saying about Jesus?

Key thought for today:

The Splendor Before...!

John 17:1-5

What was Jesus praying for in The Garden?

What is the "Splendor Before" that Jesus is asking the Father to reveal?

Key thought for today:

True Form!

John 1:1-2, 14

What is the "garment" we are called to wear?

Why do we need to prepare ourselves for His glory?

Key thought for today:

God Lasts!

Isaiah 40:27-31

When you find yourself in a frustrating situation, do you tend to try and work it all out on your own until your strength is all gone or do you immediately give it over to God and let Him carry you through?

If you have become overwhelmed in life, where can you go to have your strength renewed?

Key thought for today:

The Way Thru!

Matthew 1:20-23

What did the Israelites want to do when they came to the Red Sea and saw no way out?

You have a choice to either hold onto your frustrations or grab hold of the Master's hand, what will you do?

Key thought for today:

A Great Light!

Isaiah 9:2-7

What was the significance of Jesus coming in the form of a baby?

Why was Jesus' birth to be celebrated more than any other?

Key thought for today:

Contemplated Seed!

2 Corinthians 9:8-11

What should we do with the "seeds" God has given to us?

Are you investing in the lives of others lovingly or selfishly?

What are you planting?

Key thought for today:

Transfigured!

2 Corinthians 3:16-18

Why do you think we tend to continue to walk in darkness when we can walk in the light?

Why is it impossible to walk in darkness once you've seen the light?

Key thought for today:

Surfing Promises!

Psalms 42:6-8, 11

What happens when we focus on God despite the crashing waves we encounter in life?

Are you fully focusing on Him?

Key thought for today:

God Luck!

Psalms 32:8-11

Describe what "God Luck" really is.

Are you fully anchored in Jesus or are you being tossed to and fro without a lifeline?

Key thought for today:

Chiseled in Stone!

Job 19:23-27

Who would you like to take to Heaven with you?

What would you say to them if you knew today was your or their last day on Earth?

Why are you waiting?

Key thought for today:

Fresh Start!

2 Corinthians 5:16-20

If the old man deals in politics and blasts others and we do the same on the opposite side, then how are we shining the light of Christ?

Would God be ashamed of your actions, words, deeds?

What are you doing to shine the light of first love to those around you?

Key thought for today:

Life in You Yet!

Revelation 3:2-3, 20-21

How are you treating those around you in His love and service?

Are you so self absorbed that you think only of you and have your head under the covers of warmth and security without realizing that you are shutting others out in the cold?

Is your head so deep into your own needs and desires that you miss the moments of life He is speaking to you?

Key thought for today:

Loving Correction!

Proverbs 3:5-12

How does God discipline us?

What must we do when we find ourselves facing a "mountain of desperation"?

Key thought for today:

As Soon As...!

Jeremiah 29:10-11

What is your "as soon as"?

Pray today that God will reveal your "as soon as" to you so you might get diligent in doing what needs to be done to obtain His promise

Key thought for today:

Attention, Please!

Matthew 6:34

Where is your focus?

Ask your family, what is the one thing I cannot live without?

Key thought for today:

Act Like It!

John 13:12-17

What is holiness?

What was the cleanliness of spirit that Jesus was referring to?

How often are we guilty of the same thing?

Key thought for today:

The Faith Power!

1 John 5:4-5

How do we achieve "Faith Power"?

If we know we are the conquerors and nothing can defeat us in the power of God, then why do we walk around like a beat up, stomped out piece of dirt?

Key thought for today:

For Such a Time...!

Esther 4:12-14

We all walk through difficult circumstances in our life; Do you choose to see these as His purpose and plan?

Are you fully trusting Him To direct your path?

Key thought for today:

Time to Change!

Acts 3:19-23

What is the key to change?

How do we affect and maintain a change in our lives so that we will be ready for the return of The Messiah?

Key thought for today:

Shifting the Focus!

Romans 3:25-26, 31

What happens if we shift our focus off of our lack onto His ability to provide for us?

Key thought for today:

God's Commission!

Joshua 1:5-9

What is the key to finding the right commission that God has for you?

Do you have a personal commission from Him?

Key thought for today:

Proofed!

Matthew 11:16-19

Are you ready? Are you preparing, gathering the lost at all cost, reading and sharing His word?

Key thought for today:

Gone Hunting!

Proverbs 21:21

What will you hunt for today?

Key thought for today:

Dessert Road!

Isaiah 43:16-21

What "new things" can you see God doing for you? Taste and see that He is good!

Key thought for today:

Hurry with the Answer!

Psalms 143:7-10

We all struggle from time to time, but what makes the difference for those who are trusting and waiting for God to show up?

We may not always get the answer we want, but what is the one thing we can depend on?

Key thought for today:

Active Fire!

Hebrews 12:25-29

How do we know what will catch the flame of God versus the flames of hell?

Do you have some "junk" in your life that needs to be cleaned out?

Key thought for today:

The Confidence!

1 John 5:14-15

What brings confidence to a relationship?

Because of this confidence, what then do we have an assurance of when we ask in Jesus' name?

Key thought for today:

Seize Life!

1 Timothy 6:11-12

What kind of life are we told to pursue?

Pursuit is:

Key thought for today:

Our Knight!

Psalms 18:1-2

What makes us strong?

When you are feeling weak and at a loss of control over your situation, describe how it makes you feel when God comes in and surrounds you with His peaceful presence.

Key thought for today:

Yell No! Whisper Yes!

James 4:7-10

Did you just yell at satan? Describe what that felt like.

Go ahead and whisper Jesus' name. Do you feel his power and presence strengthening you right now? What is your perception of your day now?

Key thought for today:

Pay Day!

Proverbs 16:1-2, 9, 17, 20

What is the key to working and walking in a great life with no deductions from our pay day?

What will be the greatest "Pay Day" that we have to look forward to?

Key thought for today:

Driver's Seat!

Matthew 16:24-26

What kind of deal is it if you win in the moment but lose out in eternity? What is worth losing out on the eternal? What are some things we tend to put before God?

Sacrifice =

What did Jesus say about self-sacrifice?

Key thought for today:

Wide, Open Spaces!

Romans 5:1-2

Who has free, abundant and immediate access to God?

What does this access mean?

Key thought for today:

In Full View!

1 Chronicles 29:10-13

Why are we so secretive about our worship?

What happens when we worship and praise openly and wholeheartedly?

Key thought for today:

Chew and Pray!

Psalms 19:11-14

How do we find our way without playing the fool?

What are you chewing on? List some scriptures that you can meditate on today.

Key thought for today:

Beyond the Limit!

1 Corinthians 10:13

What do we need to remember when we feel that we are being pushed to our limit?

Key thought for today:

Displace Worry!

Philippians 4:4-7

So, what is the best way to let your worries go?

Who is your best cheerleader?

Key thought for today:

Centered!

Jude 1:20-25

How does Jude say that we are to keep a life centered in Christ?

How do we deal with those who've lost their way?

Key thought for today:

Spurred On!

Hebrews 10:22-25

What does it mean to "Spur one another on"?

Who can you spur on today?

Key thought for today:

Once and For All!

Hebrews 10:1-10

What was achieved by Jesus becoming the once-for-all sacrifice?

What must we do to be a part of this wonderful love story?

Key thought for today:

Together!

Isaiah 41:1

Time together, that's what God wants. How will you spend this time today? Sit down and tell Him what's on your heart.

Key thought for today:

Chances!

Matthew 19:17, 23-26

Can you do it? Is there a special "treasure" in your life that you are willing to give up? Pray about it, ask God to help you make a change today.

Key thought for today:

Diamond Teardrops!

James 1:2-18

Can we be joyful in times of tribulation?

How do you receive the "crown of life"?

Key thought for today:

My Very Being!

Psalms 40:6-8

What is He writing about you?

Are you listening? Seeing? Walking? Believing?

Key thought for today:

The Freedom Rule!

James 2:12-17

Are you fully committed to the faith that leads to freedom?

Who can you love through the thorns into God's kingdom today?

Key thought for today:

Oceanic Verdicts

Psalms 36:5-9

Why do we let the littlest things get us down?

How can we turn the grains of sand of irritation into pearls?

Key thought for today:

Pearl of Great Price!

Romans 8:18

What if your greatest ministry to others comes out of your greatest hurt or deepest wounds? Do you have a pearl?

Key thought for today: